# Our Father's Design

**OrangeBooks Publication**

1st Floor, Rajhans Arcade, Mall Road, Kohka, Bhilai, Chhattisgarh 490020
Website: **www.orangebooks.in**

---



**First Edition, 2025**

**ISBN:** 978-93-7426-546-8

**Price:** Rs. 349.00



Printed in India

# OUR FATHER'S DESIGN

## SEE HOW HE SEES

SATISH MYLAPORE

OrangeBooks Publication
www.orangebooks.in

# DEDICATION

To God, who opened my heart and awakened in me the desire to know Him more deeply. His boundless grace and love have been my constant guide and inspiration throughout this journey.

To my beloved wife Sathya Priya, whose unwavering encouragement and belief in me gave me the strength to pursue this vision and bring this book to completion. Her support has been my anchor.

To my Genesis Fellowship friends, who stood by me with prayers, encouragement, and wisdom, walking alongside me through this process. Their friendship and support have been a true blessing.

With gratitude and love, I dedicate this book to all of you.

# FOREWORD

Satish has taken up a complex job of undoing the confusions and misunderstandings of the Bible and ultimately misrepresenting the nature of God Himself. Honestly speaking, He has done a wonderful job at it within the span of such a small (in terms of pages) book. Instead of getting himself and thankfully us readers too, tangled in the plethora of theological jargons and debates surrounding the topic, 'How to approach scriptures?,' he offers a simple but profound approach that will illuminate our eyes and astonish our hearts at the goodness of the Father.

If you are like me who loves to do a bit of word study, this book is a treasure trough of insight into words and deeper meanings. If you like to know the historical background of things said, Satish has given the historical facts in brief strokes. Above all, he invites us to see the "Big Picture," the grand meta narrative, the storyline of the Scriptures from the vantage point of the Father. God is a master storyteller. There is a reason why the Bible is given as a narrative into our hands instead of a concordance of theological definitions and statements. The reason being we are not supposed to just analyze it with our minds but engage it from our hearts. That's what stories do. Satish invites us to see what the big picture is all about.

These days when you go into restaurants, the menu card has English alphabets printed, the names of the dishes are from native languages which we have no idea of. So, it is always helpful when the waiter stands by us and helps from pronouncing the name of the dish right to explaining what the dish is all about. Then the Master Chef prepares the grand meal, and the waiter serves us to enjoy. In some great restaurants, the chef himself comes around to find out how we are enjoying the meal. Instead of the above experience, just imagine you going into a restaurant, you trying to read the menu card all by yourself and walking out without ordering anything because you were frustrated, not understanding the words there. Sadly, that's the current state of many Christians as they read the bible.

The Master Chef (Father) has prepared a grand Meal (Christ). The Holy Spirit, the waiter and Helper, wants to help us understand the menu card (the Bible) so that we can experience the full meal (Christ) to our enjoyment and satisfaction. So, the best way to read the Bible is, to read it along with the Trinity so that we can experience the Meal to the fullest. Satish masterfully has invited us to come along a journey to do just that! I pray and hope that you will enjoy it as much as I did. Bless you

**Jesudian Silvester**

In His grip

(Lead Pastor - The Father's House, Chennai, India)

# PREFACE

Throughout history, humanity has sought to understand God, His Word, and His divine purpose. The Bible has been at the center of this quest, studied, debated, and interpreted through countless lenses. Yet, amidst theological discourse and religious traditions, a crucial question often goes unasked: How does Father God intend for us to see the Scriptures?

This book is more than just an exploration of God, the Bible, the Law, biblical history, and redemption - it is a journey into God's perspective. It challenges the traditional interpretations shaped by human reasoning and seeks to unveil how Father God sees the Scriptures He provided. It reveals how misguided traditions, and theological frameworks have led many to misunderstand the true heart of His message, drifting away from His original intent.

From the beginning of time, God has desired relationship over religion, sonship over servanthood, and intimacy over legalism. Yet, many have approached the Scriptures as a mere rulebook, an instruction manual, or a legal code rather than as a divine revelation of the Father's heart. This book reveals how God has never intended Scripture to be a rigid set of laws but rather a living testimony leading humanity to Jesus Christ, the ultimate revelation of the Father's heart and His love for us.

The Law, often viewed as a standard for righteousness, was never meant to become the means of salvation, it was always pointing to Christ. The plagues of Egypt, more than divine judgments, serve as symbolic representations of the journey of humanity's fall through Adam and the redemptive power of Jesus in reversing every loss occurred through Adam. And the Bible itself, rather than being a fragmented collection of doctrines and traditions, is God's invitation to walk in intimate communion with Him, seeing through His Spirit.

This book not only presents a theological and historical perspective but also serves as a guide to re-align how we read and understand Scripture. It challenges the false perceptions shaped by human traditions and instead unveils how the Father desires us to approach His Word, with an open heart, free from religious burdens, and centered on Jesus Christ.

As you read this book, I invite you to let go of religious traditions that have clouded your vision and embrace the Scriptures as God intended. May your eyes be opened to see what the Father sees, your heart be softened to receive what He desires to reveal, and your spirit be awakened to the truth that has always been there, God's Word is not a set of rules to be followed but a love letter leading us to know the Father.

This is an invitation to see the Scriptures through the lens of the Father God. May this journey transform the way you read, understand, and live by the Word, not as tradition dictates, but as the Father desires.

# PROLOGUE

What if we have been understanding the Scriptures through a lens that was differently intended?

For centuries, humanity has approached God's Word through tradition, doctrine, and religious structures, often interpreting it through human reasoning rather than divine revelation. Many have sought truth in the Bible, yet few have paused to ask a fundamental question:

How does Father God see the Scriptures He provided?

From the earliest days, the Bible has been studied, debated, and even weaponized, used to enforce laws, uphold religious systems, and define morality. But in doing so, have we drifted from the heart of God? Have we allowed tradition to cloud revelation? Have we sought knowledge about God while missing God Himself?

This book encourages us to rediscover the Scriptures, not through the lens of human tradition, but through the eyes of the Father. It challenges the idea that the Bible is merely a rulebook or an instruction manual, revealing instead that it is the story of God's love, His heart, and His plan for humanity's restoration.

**The journey ahead will uncover how:**

- The concept of the word "God" has been shaped by history, culture, and language, yet Jesus revealed the true nature of God, not just as a God, but as a loving Father.
- The Bible has been interpreted in ways that distance people from God, when it was always meant to bring us into intimacy with Him.
- The Law was never meant to be the ultimate measure of righteousness; rather, it served as a guidepost and mirror, pointing toward Christ and the true freedom found in Him.
- The Ten Plagues of Egypt symbolize the fall of humanity through Adam, and how Jesus Christ reversed every loss and restored what was broken.
- Traditions and religious frameworks have obscured the Father's heart, leading many to see God through fear, rather than love. This is a call to see the Scriptures as the Father intended, not as a burden to be followed, but as an invitation to relationship, sonship, and divine love.

As you embark on this journey, set aside preconceived notions. Allow your heart to be open. Ask yourself:

Have I been reading the Bible through human understanding with the knowledge of what I have heard from my traditions or have I sought to see it through the eyes of God?

The answer to this question will change everything.

**References**

Understanding some of the Biblical Hebrew roots and pictograms is crucial for gaining deeper insight into and comprehending certain scriptures. This section offers an overview of these foundational elements, providing background information on Hebrew pictograms as well as references from Strong's Concordance to aid in interpretation.

# HEBREW PICTOGRAM

Hebrew aleph-bet (alphabet) pictogram is used in this book to understand a deeper insight on the scriptures.

| Position | Name | Letter | Pictograph | Meaning | Gematria |
|---|---|---|---|---|---|
| 1 | Aleph | א |  | Ox/Strength/Leader | 1 |
| 2 | Bet/Vet | ב | 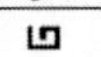 | House/Inn | 2 |
| 3 | Gimmel | ג | 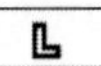 | Foot/Camel/Pride | 3 |
| 4 | Dalet | ד | 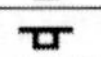 | Tent door/Pathway | 4 |
| 5 | Hey | ה |  | Lo! Behold! "The" | 5 |
| 6 | Vav | ו | 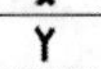 | Nail/Peg | 6 |
| 7 | Zayin | ז |  | Plow/Weapon/Cut off | 7 |
| 8 | Chet | ח | 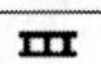 | Tent wall/Separation/fence | 8 |
| 9 | Tet | ט |  | Basket/snake/surround | 9 |
| 10 | Yod | י | 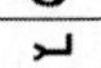 | Arm/hand/work/deed | 10 |
| 11 | Kaf | כ |  | Palm of hand/to open | 20 |
| 12 | Lamed | ל | 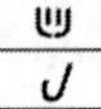 | Staff/goad/control/toward | 30 |
| 13 | Mem | מ | 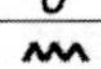 | Water/chaos | 40 |
| 14 | Nun | נ |  | Seed/fish/life/activity | 50 |
| 15 | Samek | ס |  | Hand on staff/support/prop | 60 |
| 16 | Ayin | ע |  | Eye/to see/experience | 70 |
| 17 | Pey | פ |  | Mouth/word/speak | 80 |
| 18 | Tsade | צ | 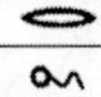 | Man on side/desire/need | 90 |
| 19 | Qof | ק | 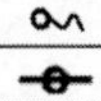 | Sun on horizon/behind | 100 |
| 20 | Resh | ר | 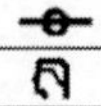 | Head/First person | 200 |
| 21 | Shin | ש | 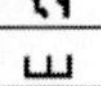 | Eat/consume/destroy | 300 |
| 22 | Tav | ת | 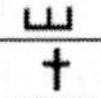 | Mark/sign/covenant | 400 |

**Fig 1: Hebrew aleph-bet (alphabet) pictogram**

The Hebrew Aleph-Bet, the ancient alphabet of the Hebrew language, originates as a pictogram system where each letter was associated with a distinct visual image and symbolic meaning. These pictograms evolved from early Semitic scripts, such as Proto-Sinaitic and

Phoenician, to the modern Hebrew script through a process of simplification and abstraction over millennia (Tigay, 2002). The purpose of this pictographic system extended beyond communication, embedding layers of spiritual, numerical, and symbolic significance into the letters. Each letter conveys a multifaceted meaning, often reflecting attributes of divine nature, moral principles, or universal truths. For example, the first letter, Aleph, symbolizes leadership or divinity, while Bet signifies a house or dwelling, reflecting concepts foundational to creation narratives. Scholars and theologians often analyze these symbolic dimensions to glean deeper insights into the Hebrew scriptures (Tanakh). Understanding the Aleph-Bet's pictorial and symbolic roots enhances scriptural interpretation by unveiling hidden meanings within the text. This integrative approach is employed in Jewish mysticism (Kabbalah) and exegetical traditions to reveal layered insights into divine wisdom and human purpose.

- *Tigay, Jeffrey H. Deuteronomy: The Traditional Hebrew Text with the New JPS Translation.*

**Strong's Concordance**

Strong's Concordance is a detailed reference tool designed to help readers study the Bible more deeply by connecting English translations with the original Hebrew, Aramaic, and Greek words. Created by Dr. James Strong in the late 19th century, it assigns a unique number, known as a "Strong's number," to every word in the original biblical texts. This allows users to locate where each word appears in the Bible and explore its meaning, context, and usage in the original language.

How and Why Is Strong's Concordance Used?

- **Word Study:** Readers can look up a specific word in their Bible and use Strong's number to trace its original term in Hebrew or Greek. This provides insight into the depth and nuance of the word's meaning.
- **Contextual Understanding:** By exploring all occurrences of a word in the Bible, readers can better understand its significance and how its meaning varies depending on context.
- **Enhanced Understanding:** Strong's Concordance is often used with lexicons or dictionaries to uncover the cultural, historical, and theological implications of a word.
- **Bridging Language Gaps:** Since translations can sometimes obscure subtleties of the original languages, this tool helps bridge the gap, enabling a richer comprehension of scripture.

Strong's Concordance is an invaluable resource for anyone seeking a deeper understanding of the Bible, whether for personal study, teaching, or scholarly exploration. It empowers readers to go beyond the surface of English translations and engage with the richness of the original biblical texts.

# Table of Content

**Chapter - 3**

**The Bible Journey**

## Chapter - 4

## Law



## Chapter - 5

## Ten Plagues Of Egypt

**Chapter - 6**

**Conclusion**



**Future Volumes**

# Chapter - 1
# GOD

## Introduction

The concept and the word "God" is among the most widely discussed, interpreted, and a controversial term in human history. Across the world, each religion, culture, and ethnic group has unique beliefs and practices centered on their understanding of God, leading to a rich diversity of interpretations. For some, God is a singular, all-powerful creator who embodies moral and spiritual authority. For others, God exists as multiple deities, each overseeing different realms or aspects of life and nature. These varying perspectives on God have profoundly shaped human societies, influencing personal faith, collective identity, and even the foundations of civilizations.

The word "God" itself has sparked countless debates, philosophical inquiries, and even conflicts throughout history. Disputes over its meaning and the true nature of divinity have led to ideological divides, cultural clashes, and even wars between people, regions, and entire nations. These tensions highlight the powerful role that the concept of God plays in shaping human thought, behavior, and relationships. The differing beliefs across religions and cultures bring forth several profound questions: What does the word "God" actually mean? How has its meaning evolved over time? And how do various groups today - both religious and secular, understand and experience this word and the idea it represents?

To explore these questions, we must take a historical, linguistic, and theological journey through the origins and evolution of the word "God." This chapter will be divided into several key sections, each shedding light on a different aspect of this concept:

1. The Evolution of the Word "God" – A historical and linguistic look at how different cultures defined divinity.

2. The Old Testament Perspective – The names of God in Hebrew Scripture and what they reveal about His nature.

3. "God" as a Title, Not Just a Name – How the Bible applies "god" to humans, spiritual rulers, and even Satan.

4. **4.** Jesus' Revelation: God as Father – Moving beyond titles to a personal, intimate relationship with God.

By examining the linguistic origins and historical context of the word "God," we can better understand its profound significance, not only in shaping religious thought but also in revealing the divine nature. With this foundation in place, we will first examine how early civilizations conceptualized God and how their terminology shaped religious thought, including the biblical understanding of the Divine.

## Evolution of the word "God"

The concept of the divine has been a cornerstone of human civilization for millennia, and early civilizations developed a rich vocabulary to describe and honor gods and divine beings. The earliest known terms for "god" can be traced to several ancient languages in the Near East, Mesopotamia, and beyond.

These terms reflect the cultures, worldviews, and religious practices of ancient people, providing insight into their beliefs and how they conceptualized the divine. Here is a detailed look at the key terms for "god" from five prominent ancient languages: Sumerian, Akkadian, Egyptian, Proto-Indo-European, and Northwest Semitic.

### Sumerian Language

The Sumerians were one of the earliest known civilizations, located in the southern part of Mesopotamia, modern-day Iraq. They developed one of the first writing systems, cuneiform, which emerged around 3200 BCE. The Sumerians were polytheistic, and their gods were deeply integrated into their daily lives, governing everything from natural forces to societal functions.

In Sumerian, the concept of "god" was represented by the cuneiform sign "Dingir" (𒀭), which was both a specific reference to a deity and a general term for divine beings. The word "Dingir" served two primary functions in Sumerian religion. It was used to signify the divine nature of a being or deity and appeared as a determinative sign before the names of gods in written texts. In this context, "Dingir" was not just a word for "god," but a mark of divinity, showing that the person or entity was supernatural. The Sumerian pantheon was vast, with gods like An (the sky god), Enlil (god of air and storms), and Inanna (goddess of love and war), each governing different aspects of nature and society.

***Reference for Sumerian Language and "Dingir"*** **(𒀭)**


- *Woods, Christopher. "The Sumerian Language in Its Socio- Linguistic Context." In The Sumerian World, edited by Harriet Crawford, Routledge, 2013.*
- *Black, Jeremy A., and Green, Anthony. Gods, Demons, and Symbols of Ancient Mesopotamia: An Illustrated Dictionary. University of Texas Press, 1992.*

- *Details on proto-cuneiform and the use of "Dingir" to represent deities can also be found in The Cuneiform Inscriptions and the Old Testament by E.A. Wallis Budge.*

**Akkadian Language**

The Akkadian was a Semitic language spoken in ancient Mesopotamia and became the lingua franca of much of the ancient Near East. It is one of the earliest Semitic languages and was used extensively from around 2500 BCE until the fall of Babylon in the 6th century BCE. Akkadian had a deep cultural exchange with Sumerian, and much of its religious vocabulary was borrowed from Sumerian traditions.

In Akkadian, the word for "god" was "ilu" (plural: "ilānu"). "Ilu" was used to refer to deities within the Akkadian pantheon, and its usage was similar to the Sumerian "Dingir." The Akkadian gods were numerous and included figures like Marduk (the god of Babylon), Assur (the god of Assyria), and Ishtar (goddess of love and war). Like Sumerian, Akkadian religion was polytheistic, with gods serving specific roles in overseeing different aspects of nature, kingship, and cosmic order.

***Reference for Akkadian Language and "Ilu"*** (𒀭𒅋𒇻)

- *Cohen, Mark E. The Cultic Calendars of the Ancient Near East. CDL Press, 1993. This book includes descriptions of Akkadian religious terminology and deities.*

- *Huehnergard, John. A Grammar of Akkadian. Eisenbrauns, 2000. An essential text for understanding Akkadian vocabulary, including terms like "ilu" for god.*
- *Studies on Akkadian deities and inscriptions are also discussed in Ancient Mesopotamian Religion and Mythology: Selected Essays by W.G. Lambert.*

## Egyptian Language

Ancient Egyptian civilization flourished along the Nile River from around 3100 BCE until its conquest by Alexander the Great in 332 BCE. The Egyptians were deeply religious, with gods associated with natural phenomena, the afterlife, and the cosmos. The Egyptian language, with its hieroglyphic script, provides valuable insights into the religious practices and beliefs of the ancient Egyptians.

In ancient Egyptian, the word for "god" was "nṯr," often pronounced as "netjer." "Netjer" referred to gods and divine beings within Egyptian polytheism. The Egyptian pantheon was vast, with gods like Ra (the sun god), Osiris (god of the afterlife), and Isis (goddess of motherhood) playing crucial roles. The symbol for "netjer" resembled a flag or a staff, which represented a divine presence or power. Egyptian gods were seen as intermediaries between humans and the cosmos, and they played roles in maintaining maat, or cosmic order.

***Reference for Egyptian Language and "nṯr" (Netjer)***

- *Allen, James P. Middle Egyptian: An Introduction to the Language and Culture of Hieroglyphs. Cambridge University Press, 2010. This book provides detailed descriptions of Egyptian religious terms and symbols, including "netjer."*
- *Wilkinson, Richard H. The Complete Gods and Goddesses of Ancient Egypt. Thames & Hudson, 2003. This reference is comprehensive for understanding Egyptian religious symbols and terminology.*
- *For the earliest inscriptions and use of "netjer," Ancient Egyptian Religion: An Interpretation by Henri Frankfort is also a valuable reference.*

**Proto-Indo-European Language (PIE)**

Proto-Indo-European (PIE) is the reconstructed ancestral language of the Indo-European language family. Scholars have reconstructed its vocabulary based on the similarities between its descendant languages, such as Latin, Greek, Sanskrit, and Old English. PIE speakers are believed to have lived around 4500– 2500 BCE, and their religious beliefs likely focused on celestial and natural forces.

The reconstructed PIE term for "god" is *"deiwos" (sometimes written as *dyēus). The PIE root deiwos is associated with celestial or sky gods. These deities were likely considered powerful, divine figures linked to the heavens or the sky. The PIE term is the precursor to words for "god" in several Indo-European languages, such as deus in Latin, theos in Greek, deva in Sanskrit, and god in Old English. The PIE concept of god reflects the early Indo-European tendency to associate divinity with celestial phenomena.

***Reference for Proto-Indo-European Language and Deiwos***

- *Mallory, J.P., and Adams, D.Q. The Oxford Introduction to Proto-Indo-European and the Proto-Indo-European World. Oxford University Press, 2006. This work includes reconstructions of Proto-Indo-European words related to deities, like deiwos.*
- *Fortson, Benjamin W. Indo-European Language and Culture: An Introduction. Wiley-Black well, 2004. This book covers the linguistic development and religious vocabulary of the Proto-Indo-European language family.*

## Northwest Semitic Languages

Northwest Semitic languages, including Ugaritic, Phoenician, and Hebrew, were spoken in the ancient Near East, particularly in the Levant. These languages are part of the broader Semitic language family, which also includes Arabic and Aramaic. The concept of “god” in these languages is crucial for understanding the development of monotheistic beliefs in the Hebrew Bible.

In Northwest Semitic languages, the term for "god" was "El" (אֵל). The term "El" was used both as a general term for "god" and as the name of a specific deity in Hebrew and Canaanite religion. “El” was regarded as the God of the gods and the chief deity, symbolizing supreme authority. The term "El" appears in Ugaritic texts (from ancient Syria), Phoenician inscriptions, and early Hebrew Scriptures. In Canaanite mythology, “El” was the central figure in the divine hierarchy, though other gods, such as Baal and Asherah, were also important in their pantheon.

***Reference for Northwest Semitic Languages and "El"***

- *Parker, Simon B., ed. Ugaritic Narrative Poetry. Scholars Press, 1997. This book contains translations of Ugaritic texts that include references to "El" as a deity.*

- *Cross, Frank Moore. Canaanite Myth and Hebrew Epic: Essays in the History of the Religion of Israel. Harvard University Press, 1973. This text explores "El" in the context of Canaanite religion and its influence on Hebrew religious concepts.*

## In a Nutshell

*In summary, the history of the evolution of the concept or the word "God" spans a wide spectrum of both monotheistic and polytheistic worldviews. In polytheistic belief systems, gods are often seen as multiple divine beings, each ruling over specific aspects of nature, society, or cosmic forces, such as weather, love, war, or the afterlife. These gods are typically part of a pantheon, where each deity has a distinct role but shares a common influence over human affairs and the natural world. On the other hand, in monotheistic traditions, God is understood as a singular, all-powerful, and transcendent being who governs everything in the universe, often associated with omnipotence, omniscience, and benevolence. Despite these differences, both viewpoints share a core concept: the idea that the word "God" (or its equivalent) represents a supreme power or divine force that exerts control over humanity and the world. This power is seen as the ultimate source of order, creation, and moral authority, shaping the lives, actions, and destinies of human beings. The evolution of the term and concept of God highlights humanity's deep-rooted desire to explain, understand, and relate to the forces that govern existence, whether through the lens of multiple deities or a singular, Supreme Being.*

**Questions to ponder**

Please ponder over these following questions and write down your thoughts

- What does the word “God” mean?
- In the Bible there are scriptures where the word “God” or “god” is associated with God, man and even on Satan.
  - Scripture that refers to God as God. Genesis 1:1 (NKJV): In the beginning God created the heavens and the earth.

- Scripture that refers mankind as God. Psalms 82:6-7 (NKJV): I said, "You are gods, and all of you are children of the Most High. But you shall die like men.
- Scripture that refers to Satan as god. 2 Corinthians 4:4 (NKJV): In whom the god of this world hath blinded the minds of them which believe not, lest the light of the glorious gospel of Christ, who is the image of God, should shine unto them.

## Old Testament view of God

The Old Testament, also known as the Hebrew Bible, is the first major division of the Christian Bible and contains 39 books (in Protestant versions). These books were written over approximately a thousands of years' period, by various authors and in different settings. Most of the texts were written in Hebrew, with a few parts in Aramaic. They were compiled into the Torah (Law), Nevi'im (Prophets), and Ketuvim (Writings), a structure known as the Tanakh in Judaism.

## Words referring to "God"

The Old Testament employs a variety of names and titles to describe and address God or Lord, each one rich with meaning and reflective of a particular facet of His nature, role, and relationship with the people of Israel. These names aren't merely labels but serve as profound expressions of God's multifaceted character, His covenantal relationship with Israel, and His supreme authority over creation. Some names highlight God's majesty and power, portraying Him as the all-powerful

Creator and ruler of the universe, while others reveal His intimate, personal connection with His chosen people, showing His role as a compassionate and faithful protector. Each name or title reveals specific attributes, emphasizing God's qualities such as justice, mercy, sovereignty, wisdom, holiness, and existence.

**El**

Among the oldest and most significant designations for God, the term "El" is widely used in the Old Testament and is rooted in ancient Semitic languages, where it traditionally conveys strength, might, and divinity. The name "El" (אֵל) corresponds to Strong's Hebrew Concordance #410 and is a foundational word in Hebrew for referencing God. In biblical usage, "El" often appears as part of compound names, each revealing a unique dimension of God's nature and character.

For instance, "El Shaddai" (אֵל שַׁדַּי), commonly translated as "God Almighty," emphasizes God's all-encompassing power and His capacity to nurture, protect, and sustain His people. This title reflects both His might and His personal involvement in the lives of His followers. Another significant compound form, "El Elyon" (אֵל עֶלְיוֹן), means "God Most High." This name underscores God's supremacy and His position above all other beings, powers, and authorities. "El Elyon" is often used in passages that speak to God's absolute authority, transcendence, and sovereignty over all creation, reinforcing that there is none greater than He.

Throughout the Old Testament, "El" functions as a standalone title and within these compound forms, symbolizing not only God's strength and majesty but also His covenantal relationship to the people of Israel. Each use reflects a reverence for God's unmatched power and His deeply personal role as protector, provider, and ruler, revealing a God who is both awe-inspiring and intimately involved in His covenant with humanity. These compound names of "El" enrich the understanding of God in the Old Testament, bridging the universal aspects of His divine identity.

**Elohim**

The term "Elohim" is a plural form of "El" and is one of the most frequently used designations for God in the Hebrew Bible, particularly in the Old Testament. It appears in the very first verse of the Bible, Genesis 1:1, where it states, "In the beginning God created the heavens and the earth." Here, the word translated as "God" is "Elohim" (אֱלֹהִים), a term referenced in Strong's Hebrew Concordance #430.

In the context of Israel's faith, Elohim consistently points to the singular, one true God. Although it is grammatically plural, Jewish tradition and Biblical usage affirm it as a majestic title for Israel's God, emphasizing the vastness and supremacy of His power, wisdom, and authority. The plural form was seen as a "plural of majesty," reflecting the fullness of God's attributes.

For Christians, Elohim also holds deeper theological significance, hinting at the complexity and unity of God's nature as understood in the doctrine of the Trinity the Father, Son, and Holy Spirit. Within Christianity, the plural form Elohim is often seen as an early indication of the triune nature of God, suggesting a unity that includes a relational dynamic within the Godhead. This understanding aligns with key passages such as Genesis 1:26, where God says, "Let us make man in our image." Here, the plural language can be interpreted as an invitation to perceive God as one in essence but existing in three distinct persons in a harmonious, divine relationship.

**Eloah**

This term Eloah referenced in Strong's Hebrew Concordance #433 (אֱלוֹהַּ), used less frequently, are singular forms that also mean "God." They appear mainly in poetic and later Old Testament books, like Deuteronomy, Job, Psalms and Daniel, showing diversity in the language used to honor and refer to God.

The choice of Eloah in certain poetic and later texts, highlights the diversity in the Old Testament's language for God. Different titles and names reflect the breadth of Israel's experiences and understanding of the divine. They present God not only as a distant, transcendent figure but as a personal being involved in human affairs and struggles. In Psalms, for instance, Eloah may be invoked to express deep worship and awe, while in Daniel, it reflects God's steadfast authority amidst foreign kingdoms and trials.

Eloah enriches the Old Testament's portrayal of God, offering a nuanced perspective that complements other divine titles. Through this singular form, the text invites readers into a more personal connection with God, recognizing both His power and His presence in the life of the believer. This term reminds worshippers that God, while vast and supreme, is also profoundly near and compassionate.

**YHWH (Yahweh / Jehovah)**

Yahweh is often referred to by the Tetragrammaton (which YHWH, meaning "four letters" word), YHWH is one of the most revered and intimate names for God in the Hebrew Scriptures. Associated with Strong's Hebrew Concordance #3068, YHWH embodies the concept of God's self-existence and eternal nature, marking Him as the unchanging, self-sustaining being who exists beyond time and space. This name is commonly translated as "LORD" in English versions of the Bible, underscoring both respect and reverence for its sacred significance.

YHWH first appears in Genesis 2:4 (NKJV): "This is the history of the heavens and the earth when they were created, in the day that the LORD God made the earth and the heavens." Here, YHWH is paired with "Elohim" (God), creating a meaningful union of God's intimate, covenantal identity with His role as the supreme creator of the universe. This combination conveys that God is both Israel's personal deity and the universal ruler of creation. In Israel's tradition, YHWH became the foundation of their understanding of God, representing His commitment to His people, His authoritative rule, and His unique, transcendent identity as their one true God.

### Adonai

The term Adonai, translated as "Lord" or "Master," is a title of deep reverence and respect, frequently used to address God in a manner that acknowledges His supreme authority and sovereignty. It is often employed in prayers, worship, and direct addresses to God, highlighting His role as the ultimate ruler and the one who governs over all creation. The use of Adonai conveys a sense of submission, recognizing God as the master and guide of life.

In the Strong's Hebrew Concordance, Adonai is listed as #136, while YHWH is listed under #3069, with YHWH Adonai generally translated as "LORD Lord" as given in the example of Psalms 8:1 (NKJV) "O LORD, our Lord." The pairing of these two terms YHWH Adonai conveys both God's personal and relational nature, as well as His supreme authority over all things. Through this dual usage, Adonai and YHWH together encapsulate the fullness of God's identity emphasizing Lord GOD as His absolute power, holiness, and intimate connection with His people.

**In a Nutshell**

*When examining the various terms used for God in the Old Testament - such as El, Elohim, Eloah, YHWH, and Adonai - it becomes clear that each word reflects a unique aspect of God's supreme nature, power, and authority.*

- *El, one of the oldest terms, signifies strength and might, emphasizing God's power over creation and His role as the supreme deity.*

- *Elohim, the plural form of El, conveys majesty and sovereignty, often portraying Him as the Creator and Ruler of the universe, encompassing both His supreme power and His relational nature with Israel.*
- *Eloah, used more sparingly in poetic and later books, underscores the intimate and personal aspect of God's presence, revealing a more approachable side to His supreme nature.*
- *YHWH (often translated as LORD) expresses God's eternal, self-sustaining existence, highlighting His covenantal relationship with Israel.*
- *Adonai, meaning "Lord" or "Master," emphasizes His authority and dominion over all things.*

*Together, these terms create a comprehensive picture of God - an all-powerful, eternal, and relational being, whose nature encompasses both supreme authority and deep connection with His people. Each name reveals a different facet of His divine essence, yet together, they weave a unified image of the one true God.*

*Yet, while these names emphasize God's divine attributes, they also raise an important question: Is "God" itself a name, or is it simply a title?*

*Throughout Scripture, the term "God" is used in different ways, not only for the one true God but also for humans and even Satan. This distinction suggests that "God" is not a personal name but rather a designation of authority, a title that signifies power, rule, or divine status.*

*While all of these titles and terms are accurate in their own right, one might wonder whether this is truly how God desires to be understood. Despite the varying names and descriptors used to convey His nature, they all ultimately point to the same divine being. Whether we approach Him as the Almighty, the Creator, the Covenant Keeper, or the Lord, all these names converge to express the singular reality of God, whose nature transcends human comprehension yet is still revealed to us in ways we can grasp.*

*While these names reveal different aspects of God's nature, the term 'God' itself is not a personal name but a title. This raises an important question: How does the Bible distinguish between God's divine identity and the use of "god" for other beings? In the next section, we will explore this critical distinction.*

## Answers to ponder

In Scripture, the term "God" is not exclusively reserved for the Almighty Creator. While it primarily refers to the one true God, the Bible also uses it to describe humans and even Satan, depending on the context. This broad application of the term can sometimes lead to misunderstanding, especially in translation.

In English, a distinction is often made between “God” (capitalized), referring to the Supreme Being, and “god” (lowercase), denoting other authorities, whether human or spiritual. However, in the original Hebrew, both are often derived from the same root words - Elohim (אֱלֹהִים)

or El (אֵל) - which are used not only for the Almighty but also for rulers, judges, and even false deities.

This overlapping usage reveals something significant: "God" is not merely a name but a title that signifies authority and dominion. The Bible, therefore, challenges us to look beyond surface-level distinctions and explore how the term is applied in different contexts. By examining biblical passages where "God" is used for humans, spiritual beings, and Satan, we gain a deeper understanding of divine authority and how it is reflected across different realms.

Next, we will explore these applications in Scripture - how the Bible refers to God as the Supreme Creator, mankind as "gods" in specific roles, and Satan as the "god of this world."

## Word "God" used for humanity

In the books of the Old Testament, the term "God" is also applied to humanity in Psalm 82. This particular psalm is traditionally attributed to Asaph, a significant figure within the Levitical priesthood and one of the chief musicians appointed during the reign of King David. Asaph is credited with composing a series of psalms, including Psalms 73 to 83, which are part of a broader collection of prayers, hymns, and songs integral to Jewish worship. These psalms, many of which date back to the era of King David, reflect the religious and musical traditions of ancient Israel.

In Psalm 82, the use of "Elohim" underscores a striking theological concept. Verse 1 opens with, "God stands in the congregation of the mighty; He judges among the gods," and in verse 6, the psalmist continues, "I said, 'You are gods, and all of you are children of the Most High. But you shall die like men, and fall like one of the princes.'" Here, the word "mighty" and "gods" both translated from "Elohim" (אֱלֹהִים) , a term most often reserved for the God of Israel, the supreme Creator. However, in this context, Elohim is applied to humanities who are expected to uphold divine justice and authority. The use of Elohim in Psalm 82 illustrates the elevated identity of humanities who were created to rule under God's covenant, bearing the image of God's authority while being reprimanded to mortality.

This choice of language links back to Genesis 1:1, where Elohim is first introduced as the Creator: "In the beginning, God created the heavens and the earth." In using the same term, Asaph points to a theological tension: those given authority on earth hold a responsibility that echoes God's own sovereign rule. The psalm declares the word "gods" to interpret humans in this context to exercise their nature with justice and integrity, reminding them that despite their elevated status, they are yet subjected to mortality.

## Word "God" used for Satan

In the New Testament, the term "god" is also attributed to Satan in Paul's second letter to the Corinthians. This epistle, written by the Apostle Paul to the Christian congregation in Corinth around AD 55-57, is one of his most intimate and intricate letters. It serves as a follow-up to 1 Corinthians, where Paul had previously tackled issues like divisions, moral failings, and doctrinal conflicts within the church. In 2 Corinthians, Paul responds to ongoing challenges, including tensions with certain community members, while reaffirming his apostolic authority. Additionally, he offers profound teachings on themes such as suffering, reconciliation, and the nature of the new covenant, aiming to strengthen and guide the believers.

In 2 Corinthians 4:4, the Apostle Paul refers to Satan as the "god of this world" or "god of this age," using this term to emphasize the power and influence Satan holds over those who are spiritually blind to the gospel. The verse reads: “In whom the god of this world hath blinded the minds of them which believe not, lest the light of the glorious gospel of Christ, who is the image of God, should shine unto them” (KJV). Here, Paul uses Theos (θεός), a term in Greek that refers to "God," which corresponds to Strong’s Greek Concordance #2316. In the Septuagint (Greek version of Hebrew Bible), the Hebrew word "Elohim" is translated as "theos" in Greek, which directly translates to "God" in English. In this scripture, however, Theos is applied to Satan, indicating his authoritative position within the world system that opposes God’s truth.

By calling Satan the "god of this age," Paul illustrates the significant role Satan plays in influencing humanity away from divine truth. This title does not imply that Satan is equal to or shares the nature of the true God; instead, it acknowledges that Satan has some dominion over worldly ideologies, values, and systems that deceive and mislead. The blindness Satan inflicts is not physical but spiritual, affecting the hearts and minds of those who reject the gospel message. This blindness prevents them from seeing the “light of the glorious gospel of Christ,” thus hindering their understanding of the transformative power of Christ, who is described as the very "image of God."

## Word “God” - Significance

Throughout history, the term "God" has evolved as a concept, consistently used to represent beings of extraordinary power and authority across various cultures and languages. From ancient civilizations to the religious texts of the Bible, this title has been applied to denote ultimate sovereignty and dominion. In ancient Sumerian culture, the term "Dingir" symbolized divine beings or deities, serving as an emblem of the supernatural forces that shaped their world. Similarly, in Semitic languages, "Ilu" was used to refer to deities, embodying the authority of the divine. Egyptian polytheism used "Netjer" to refer to gods, implying both reverence and the mystery of the unknown, while the Proto-Indo- European term "deiwos" linked divinity to the heavens, describing sky gods who reigned over natural elements and cosmic forces.

In Northwest Semitic traditions, “El” held the connotation of "God of gods," representing the supreme deity who presided over other lesser gods and was seen as a creator figure with unparalleled authority. Within the Old Testament, the words “El,” “Elohim,” and “Eloah” similarly convey reverence and majesty, with "Elohim" often used to represent a plurality within the unity of God’s nature or the expansive power attributed to Him. Additionally, "YHWH" (Yahweh) is central to the Hebrew Bible, highlighting God's self-existence, eternal nature, and His role as the personal savior of Israel. "Adonai" further enhances this understanding, translating as "Master" or "Lord," and adding the nuance of God's authority and relational presence among His people. The use of these different names captures a range of attributes, from creator to sustainer to ultimate protector.

> *"Fundamentally, the word "God" is a "Title," a designation of authority, used to acknowledge beings or forces seen as having control over specific realms and domains."*

This understanding is metaphorical to our approach to specialized fields today. For example, we recognize an orthopedic doctor as having specialized knowledge and authority within the domain of musculoskeletal health, relying on them when we face issues related to bones, muscles, or joints. Just as patients seek the expertise of an orthopedic specialist, humanity throughout history has looked to divine or semi-divine figures, labeled as "gods," for intervention in areas beyond their control or understanding. In this way, the term "God" serves as an acknowledgment of reliance on a higher power, reflecting humanity's recognition of divine authority, wisdom, and, in the case of the biblical God, a source of guidance and protection that transcends human limitations.

Thus, “God” in its many forms and uses reveals a complex understanding of humans about the divine, one that encompasses reverence, reliance, and an understanding of authority that stretches beyond the limits of human comprehension. This concept is merely a title and a testament to the universal search for connection with the ultimate, whether for guidance, justice, or understanding but never a personal relationship.

> *Addressing our Creator as "God" serves as a declaration of His divine status and supreme authority, focusing on His title and power rather than reflecting a personal, relational bond. This term emphasizes His sovereignty and majesty, acknowledging His role as the ultimate being, yet it does not inherently convey the closeness or intimacy of a relationship.*

**Summary - An introduction to the father**

*Referring to our Creator as "God" certainly acknowledges truly His supreme power, authority, and majesty. This title reflects His role as the Sovereign of all creation, the One who governs the universe with ultimate wisdom and might. However, God desires that we move beyond viewing Him as a distant, all-powerful deity and embrace a closer, more intimate relationship. As we grow in understanding of His nature, it becomes clear that He seeks to be known as "Father" rather than solely as "God." This shift from seeing God as a remote figure to relating to Him as a caring, loving Father is deeply rooted in the teachings of Jesus.*

*In the New Testament, Jesus, who is described as the "Word who was with God and was God" (John 1:1, NKJV), came into the world as the living embodiment of God. By becoming flesh and dwelling among us, "we beheld His glory, the glory as of the only begotten of the Father" (John 1:14, NKJV), Jesus revealed the very heart of God to humanity. His life was not only a testament to God's heart but also to His desire for a personal relationship with us. Through Jesus' example and teachings, God extended His invitation to each of us, calling us to approach Him not merely with formal titles but with the closeness of a child to a parent.*

*This transformative understanding is further emphasized when Jesus teaches His followers to pray, beginning with the words, "Our Father in heaven" (Matthew 6:9, NKJV). By teaching us to address God as "Father," Jesus reveals that God is not just a distant ruler but a caring, approachable presence who desires our love. This invitation to address God as "Father" opens a pathway to a relationship marked by love, guidance, and nurture, transcending the formality that often accompanies titles like "God."*

*Thus, while calling Him "God" is accurate and respectful, Jesus illuminates a deeper truth: God desires to be our Father, to draw us near, and to welcome us into a relationship where we can experience His grace, mercy, and compassion. Through Christ's example, we are invited to rise above a mere acknowledgment of His deity and step into the familial bond He has prepared for us, a bond that affirms our identity as His beloved children and He as our loving Father.*

*The word God is merely a title! If my earthly father is a Dr. I would not call him Dr. but Father.*

**Take Away**

Humanity has long been inclined to view the Creator primarily through the reverent title of "God." This perspective has been deeply ingrained in our collective consciousness, passed down through generations by family, friends, communities, and church leaders. While this reverence is rooted in deep respect, it has often led to a more formal and distant understanding of God, making it difficult for many to fully embrace Him as Father in their daily lives.

However, Jesus introduced a radical shift in perspective. In His first recorded message, He declared:

“Repent, for the kingdom of heaven is at hand” (Matthew 4:17, NKJV).

The Greek word for "repent," metanoeó (μετανοέω), literally means "to change one's mind." This was not merely a call to turn away from sin but an invitation to rethink everything, including how we see God. Jesus was leading people out of a mindset of distant reverence and into an intimate relationship with the Father.

This transformation requires more than just intellectual acknowledgment; it calls for a continual renewal of the heart. As we shift our mindset, we move beyond knowing God as a title and begin to experience Him as our loving Father. This transition is the essence of the Gospel, Jesus came not just to reveal God’s power but to restore our identity as His children.

As we embrace this truth, our relationship with God is no longer limited to worshiping a distant deity but becomes a daily walk with a compassionate and nurturing Father.

- We no longer approach Him with mere formality, but with the confidence of sons and daughters.
- We do not merely respect His authority, but we rest in His love.
- We are not just followers, but beloved children, secure in His embrace.

Thus, while we honor the title of "God," we must embrace the greater truth that Jesus revealed, that He desires to be known, not just as Creator and Lord, but as our Father. When this truth fully takes root in our hearts, it transforms how we live, how we pray, and how we see ourselves in His Kingdom. God is not a title to acknowledge, He is a Father to embrace.

## My Reflection

*This story is deeply personal, shaped by both pain and hope. My childhood was filled with struggles; I lost my earthly father at the age of 13, but even before his passing, my experiences were marked by hardship. My father was an alcoholic, which created an environment of abuse and instability that left lasting scars. Amid this turmoil, a question arose in my heart, a longing to understand if there was a Creator, a higher being who could embody the essence of a true father. I clung to the idea that if such a Creator existed, He would be everything a father should be: compassionate, loving, and infinitely a good Father with no faults or flaws.*

*Yet, despite my search for this perfect Father, the pain of my early years lingered, especially the resentment and unforgiveness I held toward my earthly father, the one person I never wanted to forgive. I couldn't imagine ever letting go of that anger. But as I came to know my Creator as my true Father, I began to experience His love and compassion, which started to transform me from within.*

*This realization of God as a perfect, loving Father opened my heart in ways I hadn't expected. In Him, I found what I had always longed for, security, love, and the embrace of a perfect Father. It gave me the strength to consider forgiveness and turned my heart to the place where I wanted to embrace my earthly father and say, 'I forgive you.' And in that moment, I understood: when we truly know God as Father, we are freed to love as He loves.*

# Chapter - 2
# THE BIBLE

## Introduction

Across history, the Bible has been interpreted through a wide array of cultural, regional, and historical lenses, giving rise to diverse understandings and practices among different communities. These distinct perspectives on biblical teachings have laid the groundwork for various Christian denominations, each of which has developed its own theological viewpoints and religious traditions. A denomination, in this context, represents a community of believers who identify with a specific interpretation of the Bible, often based on historical, linguistic, and doctrinal factors unique to their belief, region or culture. As a result, the structure and content of their teachings, practices, and liturgical expressions often differ, reflecting each group's interpretation of what they consider the central messages and values of the Bible.

This diversity of interpretation has also contributed to the development of multiple "biblical canons." A canon is a curated collection of texts regarded as authoritative and inspired within a specific religious tradition. For example, the Protestant, Catholic, and Eastern Orthodox Churches each possess distinct biblical canons, which include certain books and omit others based on their historical traditions and theological considerations. The Protestant canon, for instance, typically includes 66 books, whereas the Catholic canon encompasses additional texts known as the deuterocanonical books, and the Eastern Orthodox canon has yet other inclusions.

Despite these variations, all biblical canons ultimately trace their roots to ancient manuscripts written over several millennia. These foundational texts, composed in languages like Hebrew,

Aramaic, and Greek, have been carefully preserved and transmitted across generations. The belief in divine inspiration unites these different canons, as each religious community views their collection of sacred writings as a divinely provided guide, conveyed through individuals chosen to communicate God's message to humanity. However, the understanding of these scriptures also raises important questions: Are humans truly interpreting these texts as God intended? Does the divine message remain fully accessible, or is there deeper meaning yet to be revealed?

This chapter seeks to explore these questions by examining the Bible’s historical development, the formation of its canon, and its deeper theological significance. More than a book of laws, moral instructions, or historical records, the Bible is a divine invitation, to see God's heart, revealed through Jesus Christ, with the help of the Holy Spirit.

To fully understand the Bible's divine purpose, we must first explore how it came to be - the journey of its formation, preservation, and interpretation throughout history.

## Evolution of the Bible

An overarching perspective on the historical development and transformation of the Bible has been provided. The following discussion broadly encapsulates how the Bible has been shaped over centuries by cultural, linguistic, and theological factors.

The ancient Hebrew Scriptures that make up much of the Bible are closely connected to two significant archaeological discoveries: The Dead Sea Scrolls and the manuscripts from the Cairo Geniza. The Dead Sea Scrolls, uncovered during the 19th century in the Qumran Caves near the Dead Sea, comprise approximately 1,000 ancient manuscripts written in Hebrew, Aramaic, and Greek. These texts, dated between 250 BCE and 68 CE, include portions of nearly every book of the Hebrew Bible (except Esther), along with non-biblical writings that provide a window into the religious practices, legal interpretations, and community life of the Second Temple Jewish period. These scrolls offer the oldest surviving manuscripts of the Hebrew Bible and have been invaluable for understanding its transmission, textual variations, and preservation.

In contrast, the Cairo Geniza, discovered in the Ben Ezra Synagogue in Old Cairo, contained a staggering collection of approximately 400,000 manuscripts, including around 10,000 biblical texts. These documents, which span from the 6th to 19th centuries CE, include Torah scrolls, liturgical texts, and fragments of other Hebrew scriptures. While the Dead Sea Scrolls provide insight into the early formation of the Hebrew Bible, the Cairo Geniza illuminates how Jewish communities preserved, studied, and transmitted biblical texts through centuries of historical and cultural upheaval.

The process of compiling these ancient texts into the Bible was complex and spanned centuries. The Hebrew Bible, or Tanakh, was composed over a period of roughly 1,000 years, beginning with oral traditions that were eventually written down. These writings were preserved in scrolls, many of which were found among the Dead Sea Scrolls. By the 1st century CE, Jewish religious authorities began to standardize the Hebrew Scriptures into what is now the Tanakh. Early Christians adopted the Hebrew Scriptures as part of their sacred writings. They primarily used the Greek translation of the Hebrew Bible, known as the Septuagint, which included additional books (now known as the deuterocanonical books or Apocrypha). Over time, these scriptures were integrated into the Christian Old Testament.

During the Reformation in the 16th century, Protestant reformers chose to align their Old Testament canon with the Hebrew Bible, excluding the deuterocanonical books found in the Septuagint resulting in the 66 books of the bible in the Protestant canon.

This decision reflects the influence of ancient Hebrew manuscripts and the desire to return to the "original" texts of the faith.

**References**

- *VanderKam, J. C., & Flint, P. W. (2002). The Meaning of the Dead Sea Scrolls: Their Significance for Understanding the Bible, Judaism, Jesus, and Christianity. HarperOne.*
- *García Martínez, F. (2007). The Dead Sea Scrolls Translated: The Qumran Texts in English. Eerdmans Publishing.*
- *Hoffman, A., & Cole, P. (2011). Sacred Trash: The Lost and Found World of the Cairo Geniza. Schocken Books.*
- *Reif, S. C. (2001). A Jewish Archive from Old Cairo: The History of Cambridge University's Genizah Collection. Routledge.*

**Questions to ponder**

- What is the purpose of Father God in providing humanity with the scriptures, “The Bible”?
- Would God have provided all these scriptures if Adam hadn't transgressed?

## Common views of the Bible

The way humanity has perceived and engaged with the Bible has undergone profound changes across the centuries, influenced by the cultural norms, religious practices, and historical developments of different societies. In its earliest stages, the Bible was primarily an oral tradition, cherished by the ancient Hebrews as sacred revelations from God, providing laws, instructions, and promises. As time progressed and the texts were written and compiled, different communities began to interpret the scriptures through the lens of their own cultural and spiritual frameworks.

Some groups have approached the Bible as a comprehensive instruction manual for life, seeing it as a guide for moral and ethical conduct, spiritual growth, worship practices, and personal development. In this perspective, the Bible functions as a "life coach," offering wisdom on how to navigate relationships, overcome challenges, and live in alignment with divine principles. Passages like the Sermon on the Mount and teachings from Proverbs and Psalms are examples of texts that emphasize moral guidance and personal virtue.

Others have perceived the Bible as a legal code or rulebook, outlining a system of divine laws that dictate the boundaries of righteous and unrighteous behavior. In this view, the Bible provides clear delineations of "do's and don'ts," illustrating the rewards of obedience and the consequences of disobedience. For example, the Ten Commandments and Levitical ceremonial laws underscore Jewish understanding of God's expectations for holiness, addressing sin, transgressions, and the pursuit of righteousness. This perspective often highlights the covenantal nature of biblical laws, where blessings or punishments hinge on adherence to divine decrees.

At the same time, many have regarded the Bible as the literal Word of God, believing it to be a direct revelation of God's will and character. This interpretation focuses on the Bible's divine inspiration, as reflected in passages like 2 Timothy 3:16 (NKJV) All Scripture is God-breathed. And inspired and guided by the Holy Spirit to authors of the scripture. For these believers, the Bible transcends human writings and serves as the ultimate authority in matters of faith, worship, and salvation.

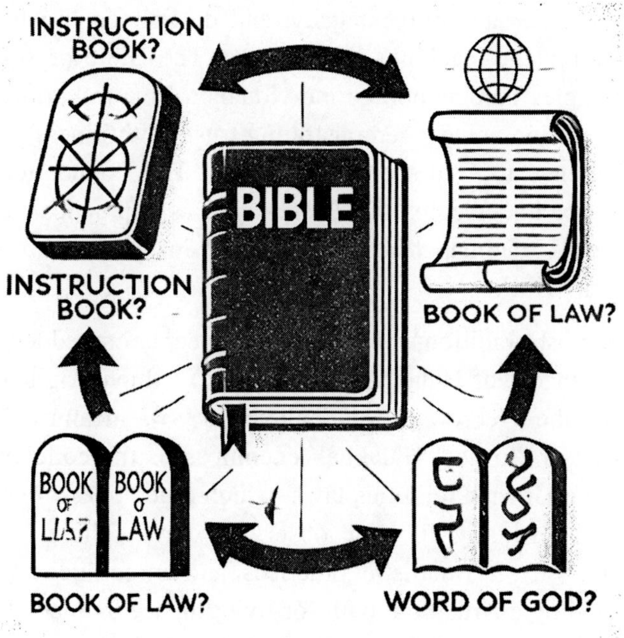


**Fig 2: Bible Views**

## Bible viewed as an Instruction book

Many have approached the Bible as a comprehensive instruction manual for life, viewing it as an essential guide for moral and ethical conduct, spiritual growth, worship practices, and personal development. This perspective characterizes the Bible as a source of wisdom and directions, offering timeless principles for navigating life's challenges and fostering a meaningful relationship with God and others.

## Principles for Right Living

The idea of living in alignment with God forms the core of understanding the Bible as a comprehensive guide for life. This perspective emphasizes the significance of righteousness, moral integrity, and disciplined living in applying the teachings of scripture. The Bible presents principles that encourage individuals to live in harmony with divine values, demonstrating trust, faithfulness, and adherence to God’s commandments. This foundational concept underscores the Bible's role as a practical and spiritual roadmap for navigating life in alignment with divine will.

In Jewish tradition, this principle is deeply embedded in the concept of Halakhah (or Halacha), which originates from the Hebrew word "halakh" (הָלַךְ), meaning "to walk" or "to go." Halakhah encompasses the collective body of Jewish religious laws, which guide nearly every aspect of daily life for observant Jews. These laws address both ritualistic practices and moral behavior, providing a structured path for living in accordance with God’s will. By following Halakhah, adherents embody the idea of "walking with God," integrating faith into every facet of their existence whether in worship, interpersonal relationships, or ethical decision-making.

In Christian traditions, the Bible is often regarded as a guide for fostering spiritual growth and leading a life of righteousness. Christians frequently refer to teachings about the fruit of the Spirit, which include virtues such as love, joy, peace, patience, kindness, goodness, faithfulness, gentleness, and self-control, as a framework for living a godly life. These qualities are viewed as the natural outcomes of a life lived in accordance with God's principles. Many biblical passages are interpreted as practical guidance for cultivating these spiritual "fruits" through righteous behavior, personal transformation, and dependence on the Holy Spirit for strength and direction.

## Worship and Spiritual Growth

The Bible often serves as an instructional manual for worship, detailing practices for honoring and glorifying God. The Book of Psalms, often referred to as the hymn book of the Bible, plays a pivotal role in this regard. It contains a wide range of poetic expressions, including songs of praise, heartfelt laments, and expressions of gratitude, which guide worshippers in articulating their faith and devotion. Psalms like Psalm 23 "The Lord is my shepherd, I shall not want" and Psalm 150 "Let everything that has breath praise the Lord" inspire believers to seek God through both joyous and challenging times, making it a cornerstone for personal and communal worship.

The Bible is often viewed as a roadmap for spiritual maturity, guiding individuals to cultivate a deeper relationship with God. Its teachings provide practical steps and principles that help believers grow in faith and align their lives with divine purpose. The epistles of Paul, such as those found in Ephesians and Colossians, are particularly rich in guidance for spiritual development. These letters emphasize critical practices such as maintaining a robust prayer life, dedicating time to studying Scripture, and fostering unity and love within the Christian community. Through these instructions, believers are encouraged to live in harmony with God's will, nurturing a profound sense of purpose and spiritual fulfillment.

By offering instructions on spiritual growth and worship, the Bible provides a framework for expressing faith through prayer, praise, and community life. These teachings foster a holistic approach to spirituality, allowing individuals to draw closer to God and live purposefully according to His will.

## Bible viewed as a Book of Law

A sect of people often views the Bible as a book of laws because it contains numerous commandments, regulations, and principles that govern moral, civil, and religious life. These laws are considered as foundational in both Judaism and Christianity, offering guidelines for righteous living and maintaining a relationship with God and others and a collection of legal principles designed to foster justice, accountability, and harmony in society.

## A Glimpse of Old Testament as Law book

In Jewish tradition, the Old Testament, also known as the Hebrew Bible or Tanakh, is viewed as a foundational source of legal, moral, and spiritual guidance. Central to this framework is the Torah, the first five books of the Hebrew Bible Genesis, Exodus, Leviticus, Numbers, and Deuteronomy. The Torah holds a unique and exalted position within Judaism, as it is considered the core of Jewish law (Halakhah) and divine instruction. It is believed to be a direct revelation from God to Moses at Mount Sinai, forming the basis of the covenantal relationship between God and the Jewish people.

The Torah is often described as both a "teaching" and a "law book," providing commandments (mitzvot) that govern every aspect of life, from personal ethics to community interactions and religious rituals. These commandments include not only moral principles, such as the Ten Commandments, but also detailed legal and ceremonial instructions, establishing a comprehensive framework for living in alignment with God's will. Through these laws, the Torah sets the foundation for the ethical and legal systems within Judaism and reinforces the sense of divine accountability and communal identity among Jewish people.

## A Glimpse to a Christian's view of New Testament as Law Book

While the Old Testament establishes the foundation of divine law, the arrival of Christ introduced a transformative shift in how the law was understood. The

New Testament presents a new perspective on the fulfillment of these laws through Christ.

The statement that Jesus brought an end to the law, as stated in Romans 10:4 (NKJV), "For Christ is the end of the law for righteousness to everyone who believes," is widely interpreted as marking the fulfillment of the ceremonial laws outlined in the Old Testament. These laws, which included ritual sacrifices, dietary regulations, and religious festivals, were seen as temporary measures foreshadowing Christ's ultimate sacrifice on the cross. With His death and resurrection, these ceremonial practices were no longer necessary, as Christ fulfilled their purpose, offering salvation and righteousness through faith.

However, this interpretation does not extend to the dismissal of all their biblical laws; many believers hold that the moral laws, such as the Ten Commandments, and civil laws designed to maintain societal justice and accountability, remain valid and essential. These laws are viewed as universal principles that guide righteous living, enforce fairness, and promote harmony in communities. They are seen as reflecting God's unchanging character and providing a foundation for how individuals can live in alignment with His will.

This understanding has led many to believe that pursuing holiness requires adherence to these moral and civil laws, which serve as a framework for ethical conduct and a disciplined life. For example, the moral directives to love one's neighbor, avoid deceit, and act justly are timeless principles that guide behavior in both personal and social contexts. Believers are encouraged to moderate their actions, thoughts, and choices according to these standards, seeing this as a way to emulate God's holiness and honor Him in daily life.

This shift in focus from the ceremonial observances of the Old Testament to living a life of moral integrity and spiritual discipline has also shaped a broader theological perspective. It transitions from emphasizing solely what God has done for humanity through Christ to exploring how humanity can respond with obedience and devotion. This response is not seen as a means to earn salvation but as a way to express gratitude, reverence, and love for God. It underscores the belief that righteous conduct and ethical living are acts of worship that please God and reflect His character to the world.

Ultimately, this approach provides a view as the fulfillment of the law through Christ to the continued relevance of moral principles. It highlights human responsibility, where faith in Christ inspires a commitment to live according to the moral and civil laws that uphold justice, accountability, and a life in alignment with God's holiness.

## Bible viewed as word of God

The Bible is also often referred to as the "Word of God," holds a central place in the faith and practice of countless believers worldwide. This designation stems from the belief that its contents are divinely inspired, serving as God's communication to humanity. Throughout its pages, the Bible itself asserts this divine origin, declaring its role as a revelation of God's will, character, and purpose.

## Bible viewed as written word of God

The Bible is widely regarded as the "written Word of God" in both Judaism and Christianity, serving as a foundational text that communicates divine truths, ethical principles, and God's will for humanity. This view stems from the belief that the Bible is not merely a human document but a divinely inspired text that conveys messages from God.

The concept of the Bible as the written Word of God became increasingly significant through the decisions of early church councils, which formalized the biblical canon by carefully evaluating and selecting specific texts to be recognized as divinely inspired. These councils sought to identify writings that authentically conveyed God's revelation and were foundational for Christian doctrine. Over the centuries, influential theologians such as Augustine and Thomas Aquinas strengthened this belief by asserting that the Bible's authority stems from its divine origin, emphasizing that it serves as God's revealed truth to humanity. During the Protestant Reformation, Martin Luther championed the Bible's role as the sole authoritative Word of God through the principle of sola scriptura (Scripture alone). This doctrine rejected the equal authority of church traditions and placed Scripture at the center of Christian faith, further solidifying its role as the ultimate guide for belief and practice in the lives of believers.

- *Pelikan, Jaroslav. Whose Bible Is it?: A History of the Scriptures Through the Ages. Penguin, 2006.*
- *Noll, Mark A. Turning Points: Decisive Moments in the History of Christianity. Baker Academic, 2012.*

**Viewed as Literal word of God**

The Bible is also described as "living and active" word of God by some sect of people where they refer Hebrews 4:12 (NKJV) where it says, "For the word of God is living and powerful, and sharper than any two-edged sword, piercing even to the division of soul and spirit, and of joints and marrow, and is a discerner of the thoughts and intents of the heart." This highlights its transformative power, penetrating deeply into the human heart to convict, comfort, and guide. It is seen not just as a historical or literary text but as an enduring, dynamic force that continues to shape lives.

**In a nutshell**

*The Bible is regarded as an instruction manual, a law book, and the word of God, showcasing its deep impact on faith, morality, and society. As an instruction guide, it provides principles for ethical living and spiritual development, with teachings such as the Sermon on the Mount and Proverbs offering timeless advice. Viewed as a law book, the Torah outlines commandments that govern moral actions, religious observances, and civil responsibilities. These foundational laws, including the Ten Commandments, continue to influence ethical behavior and societal values in both Jewish and*

*Christian traditions. Additionally, the Bible is honored as the Word of God, considered divinely inspired and authoritative. Early church councils formalized its canon, and figures like Martin Luther reinforced its role as God's revelation and the ultimate source of guidance for faith and practice. Together, these roles demonstrate the Bible's enduring importance across cultures and generations.*

**Answers to ponder**

Although the Bible addresses a wide range of topics, it is worth stepping back to consider these scriptures from Father God's perspective. Would He have provided these sacred texts for the contexts we often interpret them in? It is important to recognize that many other religions also have scriptures that offer instructions, laws, and are regarded as the words of their respective deities. This raises the question: what sets the Bible apart? How do its scriptures demonstrate their unique significance?

The Bible itself provides insight into this distinction. In John 5:39 (NLT), Jesus says, "You search the Scriptures because you think they give you eternal life. But the Scriptures point to me!" This verse highlights the Bible's central purpose: its ultimate aim is to direct humanity toward Jesus Christ. Unlike other texts that primarily focus on moral instruction or divine laws, the defining feature of the Bible is its testimony about Jesus. It serves as a roadmap leading believers to know and understand The Father God through Christ. The essence of the Bible lies in its unwavering focus on revealing Jesus as the cornerstone of faith, demonstrating that its ultimate message transcends rules or rituals it centers on a relationship with Christ.

## What does the Bible say about itself

In John 5:39 (NLT), Jesus states, "You search the Scriptures because you think they give you eternal life. But the Scriptures point to me!" Here, He is addressing the Jewish people and referencing the Scriptures that had been entrusted to them. This likely includes the Tanakh, the Hebrew Bible, which is divided into three sections: the Torah (Law), the Nevi'im (Prophets), and the Ketuvim (Writings). It may also encompass other books mentioned in the Bible but not included in the Protestant canon of 66 books, such as The Book of the Wars of the Lord (Numbers 21:14), The Book of Jasher (Joshua 10:13), and The Book of the Acts of Solomon (1 Kings 11:41), etc. These texts, authored by various individuals, are referenced within the Bible but are not considered part of the Protestant canon. Additionally, Daniel 10:21 references the "Scripture of Truth," whose author remains unidentified. Scholars and theologians interpret this as a heavenly record or divine document.

Whether the scriptures are canonical or non-canonical, authored by known individuals or anonymous figures, they ultimately serve one purpose: to point to Jesus Christ. The message of these scriptures transcends the pursuit of eternal life, emphasizing instead that their true significance lies in revealing and testifying about Jesus. This highlights the Bible's central theme, which is not just about human salvation, but about directing attention to the person Jesus Christ as the central theme of God's scripture.

Considering these scriptures, to Jesus, the Bible is a collection of scriptures that ultimately point to Him. In John 5:39, the word "scripture" is translated from the Greek term "graphé" (γραφή), as found in Strong's Greek Concordance #1124, meaning "writing," "inscription," or "document." Similarly, in Daniel 10:21, the word "scripture" comes from the Hebrew term "kethab" (כְּתָב), as noted in Strong's Hebrew Concordance #3791, which carries the same meaning of "writing" or "inscription." In both cases, the term "scripture" refers to a written record or document. Therefore, the Bible is not fundamentally intended to function as an instruction manual, a law book, or even exclusively as the Word of God. Instead, its true purpose is to serve as scripture, writings, or documents that point directly to Jesus Christ.

***Does this suggest that the Bible itself is not the Word of God? This leads to an important question that requires deeper exploration and clarification: what exactly is meant by the term "Word of God"? Is it referring to the entirety of the written scriptures, or does it point to something beyond the text itself? Understanding this distinction is crucial, as it shapes how we interpret and engage with the Bible.***

## What does "Word" of God mean?

Looking closely at the original Greek and Hebrew texts of the Bible, it becomes evident that the term "scripture" is not synonymous with the "Word of God." However, there are passages within the scriptures where the phrase "Word of God" is explicitly mentioned in both Greek and Hebrew contexts. For instance, in Matthew 4:4 (NKJV), Jesus says, “It is written, ‘Man shall not live by bread alone, but by every word that proceeds from the mouth of God.’” In this verse, the term "word" is derived from the Greek word “rhéma” (ῥῆμα), as listed in Strong’s Greek Concordance #4487, meaning "a thing spoken," "a saying," or "a command." Here, "rhéma" emphasizes a spoken or uttered word, reflecting divine communication.

In another example, in John 1:1 (NKJV), it is written, “In the beginning was the Word, and the Word was with God, and the Word was God.” The term "word" in this verse is derived from the Greek word “logos” (λόγος), as noted in Strong’s Greek Concordance #3056, which translates to "a word," "speech," or "analogy." In this context, "logos" is used to describe a deeper, more profound concept, referring to the divine expression and embodiment of God, which Christians interpret as Jesus Christ.

Examining these examples highlights an important distinction in the English translation of the Bible. The single English word "word" used in the New Testament actually corresponds to two different Greek terms “rhéma” (ῥῆμα) and “logos” (λόγος) each carrying its own unique nuance and significance. This differentiation underscores the importance of understanding these terms in their original linguistic and theological context. Recognizing the distinct meanings of "rhéma" and "logos" provides clarity in how the "Word of God" is described in scripture, enhancing our comprehension of its multifaceted role in both spoken and eternal forms of divine revelation.

### **"Rhéma" (ῥῆμα) Word of God**

Rhéma (ῥῆμα) refers to the spoken word of God, which carries the power to fulfill the purpose for which it is spoken. This concept is emphasized in Isaiah 55:11 (NKJV), where it is written, "So shall My word be that goes forth from My mouth; It shall not return to Me void, But it shall accomplish what I please, And it shall prosper in the thing for which I sent it." This verse highlights the effectiveness and authority of God's spoken word in accomplishing His will and achieving His divine purposes.

A vivid illustration of Rhéma can be seen in the account of creation recorded in Genesis Chapter 1. Throughout the six days of creation, beginning with Genesis 1:3, where God declared, "Let there be light," and light came into existence, God's spoken word initiated the formation of the universe. From separating the waters, creating vegetation, and forming celestial bodies, to bringing forth living creatures, every aspect of creation came into being through the spoken command of God. This act of speaking creation into existence demonstrates the creative and authoritative nature of the Rhéma word, as what God declared was immediately fulfilled.

In this context, Rhéma is not merely a word spoken aloud; it is the manifestation of God's will, a dynamic expression of His power, and a declaration that brings His purposes into reality. The creation narrative serves as a powerful example of the Rhéma word in action, where God's spoken commands gave life and form to the universe. This underscores the idea that the Rhéma word is more than a statement, it is an active power that accomplishes what God has determined, reflecting His sovereign authority and creative power.

**Is God the only one who can speak the Rhéma word?** The answer is no. As humans, we are created in the very image of God, and our words carry great power. This truth is reflected in Proverbs 18:21 (NKJV), which states, "Death and life are in the power of the tongue, and those who love it will eat its fruit." This verse highlights the profound impact of spoken words, demonstrating that what we say has the potential to bring life or cause harm. For believers, especially those who are children of God, the spoken word carries a unique significance. Just as God spoke creation into existence in Genesis 1, humanity also wields the ability to shape reality through the words we speak. Words can build up, encourage, and inspire life, or they can tear down, discourage, and bring destruction. This power requires a heightened sense of responsibility and awareness.

Therefore, we must exercise caution and intentionality with the words that come from our mouths. Speech is not merely communication; it is an extension of influence and intent. What we declare or utter can affect our relationships, circumstances, and spiritual lives. Understanding this truth reminds us to align our words with God's will and to speak with wisdom, grace, and purpose, knowing that the words we choose have lasting consequences, for better or for worse.

## “Logos” (λόγος) Word of God

The term "logo" originates from the Greek word “logos” (λόγος), which holds deep significance in ancient philosophy, theology, and rhetoric. In its original Greek context, logos carried meanings such as "word," "speech," "reason," or "discourse," symbolizing the expression of thought and communication. The concept of logos was central to Greek philosophy and later became a key theological term in Christianity.

In ancient philosophy, Heraclitus (6th century BCE) introduced logos as the principle of order and rationality governing the universe. He described logos as the guiding force that maintained balance in the cosmos. Later philosophers such as Plato and Aristotle expanded the use of logos, with Aristotle defining it as logic and reasoning, particularly in the context of rhetoric. For Aristotle, logos were one of three modes of persuasion, alongside ethos (credibility) and pathos (emotion). The Stoics further advanced the concept, describing logos as the divine rationality that sustains and permeates the natural world.

Today, a logo is understood as a graphical emblem or design that encapsulates the essence of a brand or organization. While its modern use emphasizes visual identity, its roots in logos reflect a broader idea of communication and meaning.

**References**


- *McGrath, Alister. Christian Theology: An Introduction. Wiley- Black well, 2016.*
- *Pelikan, Jaroslav. Whose Bible Is It?: A History of the Scriptures Through the Ages. Penguin, 2006.*
- *Harris, Stephen L. Understanding the Bible. McGraw-Hill, 2011.*


In Christianity, the concept of logos carries profound theological significance. In John 1:1 (NKJV), the term logos is explicitly used to describe Jesus Christ: "In the beginning was the Word (logos), and the Word was with God, and the Word was God." Here, logos represent the divine expression of God through Christ, emphasizing that Jesus embodies and perfectly reflects the nature of the Father. This is further affirmed in Colossians 1:15 (NKJV), which states, "He is the image of the invisible God." This verse underscores that Jesus is the exact representation of God in bodily form, making the invisible God visible and comprehensible to humanity.

The reasoning behind God stepping into the world in human form, apart from providing salvation, lies in humanity's inability to fully comprehend the Father. Since the fall of Adam, humanity has struggled to truly understand God's heart and intentions, even with the guidance of the scriptures. For example, the book of Leviticus outlines various sacrifices meant for atonement and worship, but Jeremiah 7:22 (NKJV) reveals a deeper truth: "For I did not speak to your fathers, or command them in the day that I brought them out of the land of

Egypt, concerning burnt offerings or sacrifices." At first glance, this might seem contradictory, but it highlights the heart of the Father. God's desire was never rooted in rituals or sacrifices but in love and relationship.

The fallen human mindset, clouded by sin consciousness, finds it difficult to grasp the true nature of the Father through scriptures alone. Humanity's understanding of God is often distorted or incomplete, and therefore, a tangible and personal representation of the Father was needed. Jesus Christ fulfilled this, being the physical manifestation of God and His character. Through Christ, humanity can not only understand God's heart but also see His persona of mercy, love, and purpose in action. In Jesus, the fullness of the Father is revealed, bridging the gap between God and mankind and providing a clear picture of the Father's nature and intentions.

***This is fulfilled in His saying in the gospel of John 14:9 (NKJV) "He who has seen Me has seen the Father." Logos is a way to see the Father in Jesus Christ.***

### "Dabar" (דָּבָר)"Word" of God

The phrase "word of God" is used frequently throughout the Scriptures, including several instances in the Hebrew Bible following the encounter between Abraham and Melchizedek. For example, in Genesis 15:1 (NKJV), it is written: "After these things the word of the Lord came to Abram in a vision, saying, 'Do not be afraid, Abram. I am your shield, your exceedingly great reward.'" In this verse, the Hebrew root word for "word" is "dabar" (דָּבָר),

which carries multiple meanings, including "matter," "thing," "speech," "command," or "promise."

This word “dabar” is significant because it encapsulates not only the spoken communication of God but also His commands and promises to His people. Furthermore, when the Hebrew Bible was translated into Greek in the Septuagint, the word “dabar” was often rendered using both Greek words “rhéma” (ῥῆμα) and “logos” (λόγος).

This dual translation emphasizes the richness and depth of the Hebrew word “dabar,” aligning seamlessly with both “rhéma” (a spoken word or utterance) and “logos” (a divine expression). This profound insight directly connects to the true meaning of John 1:1 (NKJV): “In the beginning was the Word, and the Word was with God, and the Word was God,” and John 1:14 (NKJV): “And the Word became flesh and dwelt among us.” These verses reveal that Jesus Christ is the “dabar” of God, He is the spoken Word (“rhéma”) and the precise and complete expression (“logos”) of the Father.

In the beginning, when God said in the book of Genesis 1:3 (NKJV) “Let there be light,” this act of speaking was an expression of His Word, which is Jesus Christ, through which all things were created. This is metaphorically confirmed in John 1:3 (NKJV): “All things were made through Him, and without Him nothing was made that was made.” Jesus, as the “dabar,” embodies both the spoken creative power of God and the divine essence through which all creation came into existence.

## In a Nutshell

## Purpose of the Scripture (The Bible)

*From the beginning, when God provided scriptures, humanity has often misinterpreted their meaning, leading to fragmented understandings. This can be illustrated by the following story:*

*A group of travelers set out to explore a mountain they had never encountered before. Blindfolded and filled with curiosity, they approached it, each touching a different part—the rocky ledge, a smooth slope, a tree, and a patch of grass.*

- *The first traveler declared, "A mountain is solid and jagged, like a wall of stone."*
- *The second insisted, "No, it is soft and slanted, like a rolling hill."*
- *The third argued, "It is rough and covered in bark."*
- *The fourth confidently claimed, "A mountain is leafy and soft, like a bed of grass."*

*Each traveler believed their interpretation was the only correct one, unaware that they had only experienced a fragment of the mountain's full reality. Had they combined their perspectives, they would have gained a more complete understanding.*

*Likewise, humanity often interprets scripture in fragmented ways, leading to misunderstandings. Some view the Bible as an instruction manual, others as a law book, and some as simply the Word of God. While these perspectives hold elements of truth, many miss the central theme that ties scripture together: knowing the Father through Jesus Christ. Instead of piecing together the fullness of God's heart and purpose, interpretations have often been limited, leading to divisions in understanding.*

## The Bible's Role in Revealing the Father

Some might wonder: Does focusing on the Father take away from knowing Jesus Christ or the Holy Spirit? This question reflects a fragmented mindset. Knowing Jesus is inseparable from knowing the Father, as Jesus Himself declared in John 14:9 (NKJV):

***"He who has seen Me has seen the Father."***

Furthermore, 1 Corinthians 12:3 (NKJV) confirms that even recognizing Jesus as Lord is impossible without the Holy Spirit:

***"No one can say that Jesus is Lord except by the Holy Spirit."***

The Father, Son, and Holy Spirit are not separate revelations but a divine unity - knowing any one of them leads to a fuller understanding of God. The Bible serves as a testimony to this truth, not as a fragmented set of laws or teachings, but as a cohesive revelation pointing us to the Father through Christ.

## Did Adam Need the Bible?

**Another important question arises**: Would there have been a need for scripture if Adam had not transgressed? The answer lies in Adam's unique relationship with God. Unlike later generations, Adam had direct, unbroken communion with the Father. Genesis 3:8 (NKJV) describes this closeness:

***"And they heard the sound of the Lord God walking in the garden in the cool of the day."***

Before transgression, Adam did not require written instructions - his understanding of God was experiential and relational, not dependent on scripture. However, when sin fractured that direct relationship, the Bible became necessary as a means of guiding humanity back to the knowledge of the Father.

## Conclusion: The True Purpose of Scripture

The Bible was given not simply as a rulebook or instruction guide for moral obligation or even to please God, but as divine revelation, designed to restore humanity's lost understanding of our good, good Father. Every passage, prophecy, and teaching ultimately serves one purpose:

***To guide us back into the relationship with the Father by knowing HIM through Jesus Christ, with the help of the Holy Spirit.***

Rather than viewing scripture in isolated fragments, we are called to see the full picture—one that reveals not just laws, wisdom, or prophecy, but the heart of the Father, who desires to be known.

## Take Away

As illustrated in the story of the blindfolded travelers and the mountain, it is easy to become distracted by the various interpretations, practices, and disciplines of humanity. While each perspective may hold a fragment of the truth, the challenge lies in striving to understand the scriptures as Father God intended and seeing them through His perspective. This has been a continual struggle for humanity since the fall of mankind. However, with the coming of Jesus Christ, we now have the ultimate revelation of Father God. As Hebrews 13:8 (NKJV) reminds us, "Jesus Christ is the same yesterday, today, and forever." Any scripture that seems to conflict with who Jesus is reveals either a misunderstanding of the scripture or a failure to fully comprehend Father God's nature.

For example, the Old Testament law in Leviticus 24:20 (NKJV) states: "fracture for fracture, eye for eye, tooth for tooth." Yet, in the New Testament, Jesus redefines this principle in Matthew 5:38-39 (NKJV): "You have heard that it was said, 'An eye for an eye and a tooth for a tooth.' But I tell you not to resist an evil person. But whoever slaps you on your right cheek, turn the other to him also." This shift in emphasis reveals something profound about the heart of the Father. Jesus, being the exact representation of God, demonstrates that the heart of the Father is not rooted in retribution but in mercy, grace, and love.

This understanding challenges us to reconsider the purpose of laws like "fracture for fracture, eye for eye" in their original context. Rather than taking such instructions literally as God's ultimate desire, we are called to dig deeper into their intent.

These laws, given in a specific cultural and historical setting and not to express the fullness of God's heart. Through Jesus, we see the true nature of the Father, a nature that surpasses human legalism and calls to love others even in the face of wrongdoing.

Thus, when scripture appears to conflict with the nature of Christ, it invites us to seek a deeper understanding of God's heart. The life of Jesus is the lens through which all scripture should be interpreted, for He perfectly reveals the Father's character. This approach encourages us not to cling to literal interpretations that contradict God's revealed nature but to seek the greater truth of His love through Jesus.

> ***Keep Jesus Christ as the center of the Bible to know the Father God, with the help of the Holy Spirit.***
>
> ***In other words, the Bible serves as a scripture to Know the Father through Jesus Christ with the help of the Holy Spirit.***

***The Ultimate***

> ***When you start knowing the Father, you will start seeing yourself as the Father Sees you***
>
> ***When you start seeing yourself as Father sees you, you will start seeing others as Father sees them.***

***In this the laws of Jesus Christ, the greatest commandment is eventually fulfilled as said in the scripture in the gospel of Matthew 22:37-39 (NKJV) "'you shall love the Lord your God with all your heart, with all your soul, and with all your mind.' This is the first and great commandment. And the second is like it: 'You shall love your neighbor as yourself.'"***

## My Reflection

***A journey of knowing the Father***

*Throughout my life, I have carried a deep longing to know the Father as Jesus knew Him. His words in Matthew 11:27 (NKJV) remained in my heart:*

***"No one knows the Son except the Father. Nor does anyone know the Father except the Son, and the one to whom the Son wills to reveal Him."***

*Despite this desire, I often found myself struggling to fully understand certain scriptures and truly grasp the nature of God. At times, it felt as though the deeper meaning remained just out of reach. Yet, I made a firm decision—to keep reading the Bible, to keep seeking, and to trust that in time, the Father would reveal His truth, even if understanding did not come immediately.*

***The Slow Unfolding of God's Answers**: As the years passed, I began to see how God unveils His answers are yes and amen, but it looked gradual, in His perfect time. Many of the questions I had carried for years were answered, but not instantly. Some took time, while others required decades of spiritual growth before I could fully comprehend them.*

*Some answers took months, others years, and a few even decades to unfold. Yet, as I looked back, I saw a pattern—God was not withholding answers but preparing my heart to receive them. The moment I had a question, He began working within me, shaping my understanding, refining my heart, and aligning my perspective so that when the answer came, I was ready to receive it.*

***God's Timing is About Growth, Not Delay**: Through this journey, I came to understand an important truth: God does not withhold understanding; He gives it immediately but we get it in the right season, when we are mature enough to grasp and cherish it. Had He given me certain answers earlier, I may not have truly valued or comprehended them. His wisdom is such that He never gives us more than we can handle at a given moment.*

*Instead of seeing delays, I started seeking to know Him. He work s patiently, guiding us through seasons of learning and transformation, ensuring that when we receive His answers, they bring not only knowledge but also joy, fulfillment, and deeper faith.*

*Today, when I encounter unanswered questions, I no longer grow restless. I trust that the moment I bring my questions to the Father, He begins preparing me for the answers. Whether they come in week s, years, or decades, I now know one thing for certain:*

*God's answers are never late - they come precisely when we are ready to receive them.*

# Chapter - 3
# THE BIBLE JOURNEY

## Introduction

The Bible has a vast collection of nearly 400,000 manuscripts, which includes around 10,000 texts directly tied to biblical writings. These texts were eventually curated and structured into what is now known as the Protestant canon, consisting of 66 books. While countless manuscripts outside of this canon are considered to be divinely inspired and hold significant historical and theological value, only these 66 books were officially recognized and canonized for their doctrinal authority within Protestant traditions. When we examine these 66 books as a cohesive unit, they present a comprehensive narrative that stretches from the creation of the world to the final Revelation of God's ultimate plan. Even though other manuscripts, though not part of the canon, often fit within the context, depth, or parallel insights that align with and enhance the broader context of the Bible. This interconnectedness underscores the unity and thematic continuity of the biblical message as a whole.

This chapter focuses exclusively on the 66 books of the Protestant canon to explore the overarching plan of the Bible. This approach provides a "bird's-eye view" of the biblical narrative, offering a cohesive understanding of its overarching themes and purpose. Through this broader perspective, questions such as why the Israelites were chosen as God's special people and the significance of their covenant relationship come to light. It also addresses common misconceptions, such as the belief that God's expulsion of Adam and Eve from the Garden of Eden was an act of anger, rather than an event shaped by divine respect and love.

Understanding this overarching narrative is essential for grasping the unity and depth of the scripture. It reveals how each part of the Bible fits within a grand design, spanning from creation to the ultimate restoration of divinity in humanity. This broader perspective not only clarifies the Bible's narrative arc but also illuminates the character of God His unwavering love, mercy, and desire for a restored relationship with His creation. By considering the Bible through this lens, the beauty and intentionality of God's plan become apparent, inviting deeper reflection and appreciation.

## Journey

The central theme of the Bible, Creation, Fall, Redemption, and Restoration serves as the foundation for understanding its overarching narrative. By following this theme in a linear progression, beginning with the account of creation, the purpose behind God’s act of bringing the universe into existence can be explored in depth. This journey continues through humanity's fall into transgression, examining its profound implications on the relationship between God and His creation. From there, it delves into the unfolding plan of redemption, culminating in the life, death, and resurrection of Jesus Christ, which serves as the cornerstone of God’s promise to restore all things. Finally, it reaches the ultimate restoration of God’s kingdom, where all creation is reconciled and renewed.

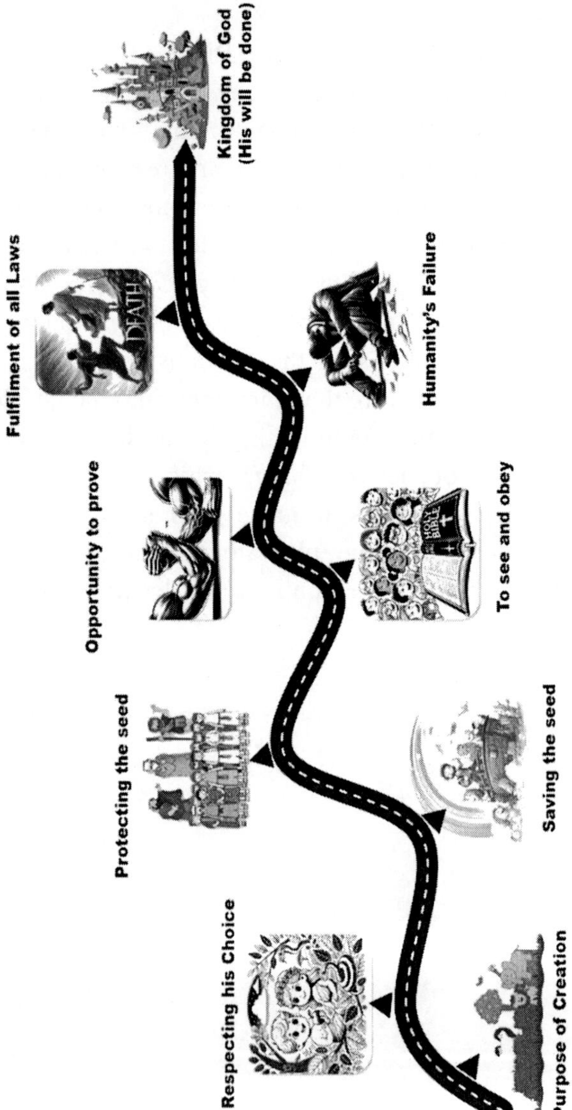


**Fig 3: Bible Journey**

**Questions to ponder**

- Does the Bible have a storyline?

## Purpose of Creation

The Bible is being used to present a multifaceted understanding of humanity's purpose, including reflecting God's image, glorifying and worshiping Him, loving Him and others, stewarding creation, and participating in His eternal plan. Humanity was uniquely created to embody God's character and to honor and partner with Him through relationship. Loving God wholeheartedly and showing His love to others are central themes, alongside the responsibility to care for the earth as stewards of His creation.

God's existence is eternal, transcending the boundaries of time and space. He existed before the creation of the universe and remains constant and unchanging throughout eternity. Unlike finite beings, God is not bound by time or dependent on anything external to sustain Him. His self-sufficiency is profoundly expressed in Colossians 1:17 (NKJV): "in Him all things consist." This reveals that all of creation is held together and sustained by His power, emphasizing that He is the source and foundation of all existence.

Furthermore, God's omnipotence is declared in Isaiah 44:6 (ERV): "The Lord is the King of Israel. The Lord All-Powerful." As the sovereign and all-powerful Creator, God rules over all with unparalleled authority and strength. Despite being entirely self- sufficient, needing nothing from anyone, His divine nature is marked by an extraordinary desire for relationship. God, in His infinite love and wisdom, chose to create humanity, not out of necessity, but out of a yearning to share a personal and intimate connection with beings made in His image.

This longing for a relationship reflects the heart of God's purpose for creation. In His desire to form a family, God brought humanity into existence, crafting mankind to reflect His image and to live in fellowship with Him. This marks the beginning of the human story, a story rooted in God's love and His desire to dwell with His creation as a Father among His children. The existence of mankind, therefore, is not merely an act of divine power but a manifestation of God's eternal plan to share His love, grace, and glory with those created to know and enjoy Him forever.

## Decision Making

Making decisions is one of the most challenging and essential aspects of life, influencing every facet of existence. It applies universally, whether to simple daily choices, significant financial planning, or any other domain requiring thoughtful judgment. The ability to prioritize and make effective decisions is a cornerstone of personal and professional success, as it impacts outcomes and shapes the future.

In the professional sphere, one effective tool for decision-making is the Eisenhower Matrix, named after the esteemed former U. S. President Dwight D. Eisenhower. This strategic framework is specifically designed to aid individuals in managing their tasks and responsibilities by categorizing them according to their urgency and importance. It provides a structured method for prioritization, enabling users to identify critical tasks that need immediate attention, schedule important but non-urgent activities, delegate less significant urgent tasks, and eliminate unnecessary distractions. The primary advantage of this tool is its ability to help individuals and humanity at large concentrate on the most critical and high-priority tasks. It ensures that time and energy are devoted to pursuits that deliver the greatest value, both immediately and in the long term.

Numerous tools and techniques are available to support and enhance the efforts of humanity in managing priorities and creating space for meaningful pursuits. A fascinating perspective to consider is how humanity, with its finite abilities, devices these frameworks and technologies to focus on what truly matters. If humans put such effort into tools that help them align their goals and passions, imagine the depth of planning and intentionality involved when our all-powerful God provided us with the Bible.

As the Creator of the universe, God, who possesses infinite wisdom and understanding, would have taken into account countless factors before delivering the Holy Scriptures to humanity. Every verse, every chapter, and every word in the Bible is purposeful, forming part of His grand design to guide, teach, and redeem His creation. This deliberate consideration becomes even more profound when reflecting on the very first verse of the Bible in the book of Genesis 1:1 (NKJV) “In the beginning, God created the heavens and the earth.”

The significance of this opening statement cannot be overstated. Out of all the truths and revelations contained within the Bible, God chose these words to introduce His divine message. This verse not only sets the foundation for the rest of Scripture but also declares His sovereignty, creativity, and ultimate love over all existence. It signals the beginning of His plan for humanity, encapsulating the profound relationship between the Creator and His creation.

## God’s Heart

The Bible is filled with numerous verses that declare God's preeminence, omnipotence, and sovereignty, all of which are undeniably true about His nature. Passages like "I am Almighty God" or "In Him all things consist" unequivocally showcase His power and authority. However, it is significant that God, in His infinite wisdom, did not choose to begin His divine revelation with such statements. Instead, He chose to open the Bible with a simple yet profound verse in Genesis 1:1 (NKJV): "In the beginning, God created the heavens and the earth."

To uncover the deeper meaning of Genesis 1:1, it is essential to return to the original language in which it was written, “Hebrew.” This ancient and richly expressive language reveals nuances and layers of understanding that may be less apparent in translation. The opening verse of the Bible, which introduces the act of creation, consists of precisely seven Hebrew words. This brevity is profound, as each word is packed with meaning and intention, forming a complete and perfect statement.

By closely examining each of these seven words, we embark on a journey to unravel the mysteries and insights that lie beneath the surface of this foundational text. These words, chosen with divine precision, not only describe the creation of the heavens and the earth but also reveal the nature, power, and purpose of the Creator Himself. Through this exploration, the verse's deeper truths come alive, offering a glimpse into the divine wisdom and intentionality behind the very beginning of all things.

## In the beginning

The first word of Genesis 1:1 in Hebrew, בְּרֵאשִׁית (bereishit), holds profound significance. According to Strong's Hebrew Concordance #7225, the word reshith is translated as "beginning" and conveys meanings such as "beginning," "first," or "chief." This term originates from the root Hebrew word ראש (rosh), referenced in Strong's Concordance #7218, which means "head," "chief," "top," "beginning," or "leader."

The root word rosh suggests the idea of primacy and leadership, emphasizing something or someone at the forefront. This concept aligns with the New Testament depiction of Jesus Christ as the "head" over all things. For example, in Ephesians 1:22 (NKJV), it is written: "And He put all things under His feet, and gave Him to be head over all things to the church." Here, Jesus is described as the ultimate leader and authority, positioned as the "head" of the church and creation.

Considering this connection, the Hebrew word (bereishit) could be interpreted in a Christocentric light, implying "In Jesus" as the starting point of all things. This interpretation reinforces the understanding that creation itself begins and exists through Him, as echoed in Colossians 1:16-17 (NKJV): "For by Him all things were created that are in heaven and that are on earth... And He is before all things, and in Him all things consist." Thus, the very first word of Scripture not only introduces the concept of a beginning but also subtly points to Jesus Christ as the foundational source and head of creation, underscoring His divine role in the unfolding story of the Bible.

## Created

In Genesis 1:1 the second Hebrew word בָּרָא (bara'), which is translated as "created." This word carries profound significance, encapsulating the divine act of bringing something into existence. Rooted in the concept of creation, bara' also conveys meanings such as "to create," "shape," and "form," emphasizing an intentional and purposeful act of crafting something entirely new
This same term is used later in Genesis 1:27 (NKJV): "So God created man in His own image." Here, the word bara' describes the creation of humanity, highlighting the unique and intentional way God formed mankind to reflect His image. This connection between the act of creation in Genesis 1:1 and the formation of humanity in Genesis 1:27 showcases the unparalleled creative power of God, who not only brought the universe into existence but also infused humanity with His likeness and purpose.

The use of bara' in these contexts underscores God's sovereignty as the ultimate Creator. Unlike human creativity, which is often limited to reshaping or repurposing existing materials, the divine act of bara' signifies creation ex nihilo, i.e., bringing something into being from nothing. This word reveals the boundless power of God to shape the cosmos, form life, and establish order, all according to His will and design. Through bara', the Bible introduces us to a Creator whose power is unmatched, whose acts are purposeful, and whose creation reflects His glory and majesty.

## God

In Genesis 1:1, the third Hebrew word, אֱלֹהִים (Elohim), emerges as a powerful and significant term. This word, translated as "God," is rich in meaning and provides intense insights into the nature of the Creator. Interestingly, Elohim is a plural noun, a unique feature that invites deeper exploration. While the plural form could imply majesty or greatness, in the context of biblical theology, it is widely understood to point to the Triune God, the Father, the Son (Jesus Christ), and the Holy Spirit.

In this context, Elohim underscores the divine collaboration within the Godhead. The Father, the Son, and the Spirit empowers, together orchestrating the creation of all things. The choice of this term in the very first verse of Scripture serves as a testament to the unity and majesty of God, reminding us that all of creation exists for Him and is a reflection of His divine nature and eternal plan.

## Untranslatable mark

In Genesis 1:1, the fourth Hebrew word, אֶת (et), stands out as a fascinating and significant element of the text. Though often referred to as an "untranslatable mark," this word carries significant meaning when examined closely. Composed of two Hebrew letters א (aleph), the first letter of the Hebrew alphabet, and ת (tav), the last, it forms a word that encapsulates the entirety of the Hebrew alphabet. Its placement and structure invite a deeper exploration into its symbolic and theological significance.

Unlike other words in the Bible, אֶת "et" has never been translated into other languages, as its meaning eluded scholars during the Old Covenant period. The Hebrew sages, though deeply knowledgeable, could not fully grasp its purpose, leaving it as a linguistic mystery. However, the New Testament sheds light on this enigmatic word through the words of Jesus Christ in Revelation 22:13 (NKJV): "I am the Alpha and the Omega." Here, Jesus identifies Himself as the Alpha and the Omega, using the first and last letters of the Greek alphabet to describe His eternal and encompassing nature. This declaration parallels the significance of "et," connecting it directly to Jesus Christ as the embodiment of divine completeness.

Positioned at the center of the opening verse, "et" serves as a bridge between the Creator and the creation. The first three words of Genesis 1:1 focus on the Creator, while the next three describe the creation itself. The placement of "et" in the middle symbolizes its role as a

Lord and mediator, binding these two realms together. This aligns with the New Testament depiction of Jesus as the mediator between God and humanity, 1 Timothy 2:5 (NKJV) “For there is one God and one Mediator between God and men, the Man Christ Jesus,” emphasizing His role in reconciling creation to the Creator.

The profound symbolism of “et” reveals its deeper theological meaning: it represents Jesus Christ, the Alpha and Omega, the beginning and the end. As the Word through whom all things were made, John 1:3 (NKJV) “All things were made through Him, and without Him nothing was made that was made,” Jesus is both the source and the purpose of creation. This untranslatable mark, nestled within the very first verse of the Bible, subtly yet powerfully points to the central role of Christ in the divine plan, highlighting His position as the ultimate link between God and His creation.

- *Several sources reference the connection between Aleph-Tav and Alpha-Omega, although the original author of this interpretation remains unidentified.*

## The Heavens

Genesis 1:1, fifth Hebrew word, הַשָּׁמַיִם (shamayim), captures a profound element of creation: the heavens. According to Strong’s Hebrew Concordance #8064, this term is translated as "heavens," "sky," or "space." Notably, the word shamayim is plural, signifying "heavens" rather than a singular "heaven." This plurality conveys not only the vastness and layers of the celestial realms that God brought into being at the dawn of creation, but also God's mystical wisdom for each of them.

The concept of multiple heavens is further reinforced in Deuteronomy 10:14 (NKJV), which states, "Indeed heaven and the highest heavens belong to the Lord your God." This verse suggests a hierarchy or multiplicity of heavens, with the "highest heavens" referring to the divine dwelling place of God and it also represents a place or a space to keep celestial objects like earth into it.

Additionally, the "highest heavens" denote a spiritual dimension beyond human observation, a realm that serves as the dwelling place of God. This exalted realm is often understood as the seat of divine love, emphasizing God's transcendence and sovereignty over all creation. The distinction between these heavens points to a universe that is both material and spiritual, each layer with its unique role and purpose within God's overarching plan.

### And

In Genesis 1:1, the sixth Hebrew word, וְאֵת (wə·'ê<u>t</u>), holds layers of meaning that contribute to the richness of the creation narrative. This word is commonly translated as "and," indicating a connection between the heavens and the earth. However, a closer examination reveals deeper insights. The root of wə·'ê<u>t</u> is the Hebrew word אֵת (et), which is identified in Strong's Hebrew Concordance #853 as an "untranslatable mark." In this instance, the word "et" is prefixed with the Hebrew letter

וְ (vav), which functions as a conjunction, transforming the word into wə·'êṯ, meaning "and."

This seemingly simple conjunction carries significant theological implications. First, the root word "et" can be seen as a symbolic reference to Jesus Christ. In this context, the presence of et before "heavens" and "earth" in Genesis 1:1 suggests that both were created through and in Jesus Christ, aligning with the New Testament assertion in Colossians 1:16 (NKJV): "For by Him all things were created that are in heaven and that are on earth."

Secondly, the addition of the hebrew letter vav as a conjunction in wə·'êṯ highlights the ordered relationship between the heavens and the earth. It signifies their simultaneous creation and interconnectedness within God's divine plan. The use of wə·'êṯ in this verse underscores the unity and harmony between the two realms, emphasizing their deliberate design and purpose.

This single word, wə·'êṯ, encapsulates both the theological depth of creation and the precise order in which God brought the heavens and the earth into existence. It bridges the physical and spiritual dimensions, symbolizing Jesus Christ as the central figure through whom all things were made, while also serving as a conjunction that ties the two realms together in perfect harmony. Through this intricate word, Genesis 1:1 subtly points to the profound relationship between the Creator, His creation, and the ultimate mediator, Jesus Christ.

## The Earth

In Genesis 1:1, the seventh and final Hebrew word, הָאָרֶץ (erets), holds significant meaning as it completes the first sentence of the Bible. According to Strong's Hebrew Concordance #776, this word is translated as "earth," "land," or "ground." Its placement in the verse emphasizes the creation of the physical world, underscoring God's sovereignty over all that exists. However, the term "erets" also carries symbolic connotations throughout Scripture, often representing humanity in a metaphorical sense.

One striking example is found in Jeremiah 22:29 (NKJV), which declares, "O earth, earth, earth, hear the word of the Lord!" While this verse directly addresses the earth, it implicitly calls upon humanity, generations, and peoples to heed God's message. The repetition of "earth" three times amplifies the urgency and universality of the command, drawing a connection between mankind and the ground from which humanity was formed. This connection is rooted in the creation narrative itself, where man is shaped from the dust of the earth (Genesis 2:7), symbolizing a profound relationship between humanity and the physical world, "the earth."

### In a Nutshell

*When we consider the meanings of the seven Hebrew words in Genesis 1:1, a profound and mysterious narrative emerges. The phrase "In the beginning" can be understood as "In Jesus Christ," pointing to Him as the eternal origin and foundation. The term "God" refers to the triune nature of the Creator, the Father, the*

*Son, and the Holy Spirit. The word "Created" signifies bringing into existence with intentionality and purpose. The Hebrew word "et," symbolizing "through Jesus Christ, our Lord and mediator," serves as the connection between the Creator and creation. The term "the heavens" describes a realm or space prepared by God, while "the earth" symbolically represents humanity.*

*When these meanings are unified, Genesis 1:1 can be paraphrased as: "In Jesus Christ, Triune God created a place (heavens) and brought mankind (earth) into it." This encapsulates the essence of the creation story in Genesis 1-2. It reveals a Creator who not only brings the cosmos into being but also designs it as a home for humanity.*

*The purpose behind this act of creation (Genesis 1:1) becomes clearer in Genesis 3:8 (NLT), which states, "When the cool evening breezes were blowing, the man and his wife heard the Lord God walking about in the garden." This verse paints a vivid picture of God's intimate relationship with Adam and Eve, suggesting that He regularly visited them during the cool of the day to commune with them. This act of fellowship highlights the Creator's intention in forming the earth (which is humanity) and placing them in a dwelling space (heaven) where He could enjoy a deep and loving relationship with humanity.*

*This understanding of creation reflects the heart of God. It shows that the earth was not merely a random construct but a deliberate design to foster connection, love, and communion with mankind. This narrative expresses God's desire for sweet fellowship with humanity, a theme that resonates throughout the scriptures, revealing His unwavering pursuit of relationship with His humanity.*

*God's decision to make this statement the very first verse of the Bible reflects its profound significance and the priority He places on His relationship with humanity. This opening declaration in Genesis 1:1 serves as more than a statement of creation, it reveals God's ultimate desire to connect with His creation. By placing this verse at the very start, He underscores the importance of fellowship with mankind as a cornerstone of His divine plan.*

*However, this does not imply that God is dependent on humanity or that He needs us to complete Himself. As the self-sufficient and eternal triune God, The Father, Son, and Holy Spirit, He exists in perfect harmony and fullness within Himself. Rather, His desire for fellowship is an outpouring of His love, not out of necessity but out of His abundant love. He created humanity with the intention of inviting us into this divine relationship, calling us to be part of His family as beloved children.*

*This invitation reflects the heart of God, Our Creator who, despite His omnipotence, yearns for His creation to experience the fullness of love and unity found within the triune Godhead. By making this verse the opening of Scripture, God reveals His purpose: to establish a relationship where humanity can know Him, walk with Him, and be a part of His eternal family. This foundational truth sets the tone for the rest of the Bible, weaving a narrative of God's relentless pursuit of relationship with those He lovingly created.*

## Respecting his choice

A widespread interpretation regarding the transgression of Adam and Eve suggests that after they ate from the tree of the knowledge of good and evil, God immediately cursed them and expelled them from the Garden of Eden. This understanding stems from the warning He gave beforehand, as recorded in Genesis 2:16-17 (NKJV): "And the Lord God commanded the man, saying, 'Of every tree of the garden you may freely eat; but of the tree of the knowledge of good and evil you shall not eat, for in the day that you eat of it you shall surely die.'" This command highlights the gravity of disobedience, emphasizing the severe consequences associated with eating from the forbidden tree. Many interpret these verses to mean that God's judgment was swift and punitive because Adam and Eve defied a direct command, despite having been granted abundant freedom to eat from every other tree in the garden. Their act of disobedience marked a turning point, introducing sin and separation into the human story.

Did you know that the Bible does not contain any verse stating that God was angry with Adam or Eve? While the consequences of their disobedience are clearly outlined in Genesis 3, God never expresses anger toward them. Instead, the word "curse" is carefully used, but not directed at Adam or Eve themselves.

The first instance of the word "curse" is found in Genesis 3:14 (NKJV), where God addresses the serpent, saying: “You are cursed more than all cattle.” Here, the curse is explicitly and directly pronounced upon the serpent, symbolizing Satan, as a consequence of deceiving Eve.

The second occurrence of the word "curse" is in Genesis 3:17 (NKJV), where God speaks to Adam, saying: “Cursed is the ground for your sake.” Notably, this curse is placed on the ground, not on Adam himself. This distinction is significant, as Adam was created in the image of God, and God did not curse His own image. The curse on the ground serves as a consequence of Adam's transgression, introducing toil and hardship into his labor.

When it comes to Eve, while some might assume she was cursed, a closer examination reveals otherwise. God never uses the word "curse" when addressing Eve. Instead, two specific areas are mentioned: the increase of pain in childbirth and her desire for her husband (Genesis 3:16). These are not curses but rather prophetic statements that carry deeper spiritual meaning.

The pain in childbirth can be understood as a metaphor pointing to the work of Jesus Christ. Just as labor pains bring forth new life, Christ bore the "birth pangs" of suffering on the cross to bring eternal life to humanity. Similarly, the desire for her husband can be seen as a reflection of the believer’s yearning for Christ, who is often depicted as the Bridegroom in the Scripture. These prophetic elements highlight God’s redemptive plan, where the consequences of the fall ultimately point toward the work of Jesus Christ and His mission to restore humanity to fellowship with God.

Thus, the narrative of Genesis 3 reveals not a God of anger but a God of love, who enacts consequences while preparing the way for redemption. Far from cursing Adam and Eve, God's response underscores His love and His commitment to restoring His creation through the work of Christ.

**Choice and Freewill**

Throughout the Scriptures, there are numerous instances where God emphasizes choice, underscoring the free will granted to humanity. One powerful example can be found in Deuteronomy 30:19 (NKJV), where God declares: "I call heaven and earth as witnesses today against you, that I have set before you life and death, blessing and cursing; therefore choose life, that both you and your descendants may live." This verse not only highlights the freedom God gives mankind to make decisions but also reflects His desire for humanity to choose the path of life and blessing.

What is remarkable about this divine approach is that, even though mankind is God's creation, He does not impose His will upon them or treat them as mere objects of His power. Instead, He honors humanity with dignity, respecting their ability to make choices as beings created in His image. This image of God within mankind includes the capacity for reasoning, decision- making, and accountability, all of which are integral to the gift of free will.

In the above scripture, God explicitly lays out two paths, life and death, blessing and cursing, while gently urging His people to choose life. Yet, He refrains from coercing or compelling them, demonstrating His respect for their autonomy. By presenting the choice and its consequences clearly, God reveals His heart: He desires for humanity to live in harmony with Him and to experience the fullness of His blessings. However, He does not override their freedom to choose, for love and obedience have true meaning only when freely given.

This invitation to choose is not merely a test of loyalty but a profound demonstration of God's relational nature. It reveals a Creator who seeks a willing partnership with His creation, valuing their decisions and offering them the opportunity to align their lives with His purpose. This respect for human free will reflects the depth of God's love and His desire for a genuine relationship with those He has made.

**Life - A Choice to Earn or A Free Gift**

When God created the heavens, the earth, and all living things, including Adam and Eve, He prepared the Garden of Eden as a place of beauty and abundance. As described in Genesis 2:8 (NKJV), "The Lord God planted a garden eastward in Eden, and there He put the man whom He had formed." God placed Adam in the garden to care for it and gave him freedom to enjoy its fruits, except from the tree of the knowledge of good and evil. He commanded Adam in Genesis 2:16-17 (NKJV): "Of every tree of the garden you may freely eat; but of the tree of the knowledge of good and evil you shall not eat, for in the day that you eat of it you shall surely die." In Genesis 3, the transgression of Adam and Eve is detailed as they succumbed to the serpent's temptation and ate from the tree God commanded man not to eat.

**Element of Goodness**

One of the most thought-provoking questions about the Tree of the Knowledge of Good and Evil is this: If the tree contains an element of goodness, then it is not purely evil. Why, then, would eating from it result in such dire consequences? To further complicate the question, we know from Scripture that God is not interested in the death of anyone, not even the wicked. This is powerfully stated in Ezekiel 18:23 (NKJV): "Do I have any pleasure at all that the wicked should die?" says the Lord God, "and not that he should turn from his ways and live?"

If God, in His infinite mercy, takes no pleasure in the death of those who are wicked and rebellious, how much less would He desire the death of Adam and Eve, His first-created beings, made in His image and placed in the Garden of Eden? God's character, as revealed throughout the Bible, is one of justice, love, and a deep longing for His creation to walk in righteousness and life, not destruction.

Furthermore, the "wicked" referred to in Ezekiel had been given the law to guide them, a clear framework to distinguish right from wrong. They knowingly chose their path, aware of the consequences. In contrast, Adam and Eve, at the time of their transgression, were in a state of innocence. They had no knowledge of good and evil, no understanding of moral distinctions. Without such knowledge, they could not fully comprehend the weight of their disobedience or the consequence of death that God warned about in Genesis 2:17. Their lack of understanding raises an important question: How could they be held accountable in the same way as those who knowingly transgressed?

This dilemma points to the profound difference between transgression born out of ignorance and rebellion carried out with full knowledge. It underscores the complexity of the fall and the merciful nature of God, who always is loving as evidenced in the plea of Ezekiel: God desires not death, but that people turn from their ways and live. This same love would undoubtedly extend to Adam and Eve, who lacked the discernment of good and evil when they chose to eat from the tree.

### Forgiving nature of God

Another profound question arises: How can a man who lacks knowledge of good and evil, such as Adam at the time of his transgression, be subjected to death? Adam and Eve, in their state of innocence, had no understanding of the moral weight behind their actions when they ate from the Tree of the Knowledge of Good and Evil. Without the ability to discern right from wrong, how could they fully comprehend the consequence of death that God had warned about?

The heart of God's mercy and justice is vividly displayed through the life and actions of Jesus Christ. This is particularly evident in His prayer during the crucifixion, as recorded in Luke 23:34 (NKJV): "Then

Jesus said, 'Father, forgive them, for they do not know what they do.'" Even in the midst of unimaginable suffering, Jesus pleaded with the Father to forgive those responsible for His crucifixion, recognizing their ignorance and lack of understanding. They did not grasp the full extent of their actions or the identity of the One they were condemning.

This moment on the cross reveals the depth of God's compassion and His readiness to forgive those who act without knowledge. If Jesus, the perfect embodiment of God's love, could intercede for the forgiveness of those who crucified Him, how much more would God, in His mercy, consider the innocence of Adam and Eve? Their disobedience was not born out of malice or rebellion but out of deception and a lack of understanding of good and evil.

This perspective emphasizes that God's judgment is not harsh or unjust but is always tempered with His profound love and desire for restoration. The same heart of forgiveness seen in Christ on the cross reflects God's nature toward humanity, even from the beginning of creation. It challenges the notion of a wrathful God and instead highlights a compassionate Creator who seeks reconciliation and understanding with His creation.

### Deliver from death

Finally, consider this crucial point: Adam did not even know what death truly was. At the time of his transgression, he lacked the understanding necessary to fully grasp the weight of the consequence that had been warned, "You shall surely die" (Genesis 2:17). How could Adam comprehend something he had never seen, experienced, or even understood? This raises a compelling question about God's mercy and justice in such circumstances.

To further illuminate this, we can look to the story of Nineveh in the Book of Jonah. When God saw the wickedness of the city, He sent Jonah to proclaim a message of repentance. Despite their sinful ways, God expressed profound pity for the people of Nineveh, saying in Jonah 4:11 (NKJV): "And should I not pity Nineveh, that great city, in which are more than one hundred and twenty thousand persons who cannot discern between their right hand and their left, and much livestock?" The people of Nineveh were spiritually ignorant, unable to discern right from wrong. Yet, when they repented, God in His compassion spared them from destruction.

If God was willing to show mercy to the people of Nineveh, who acted in ignorance, would He not also extend similar compassion to Adam and Eve? Their disobedience was not born of defiance but from deception and a lack of understanding. They could not fully comprehend the gravity of their actions, much less the concept of death itself. Just as God did not desire the destruction of the Ninevites, it aligns with His character that He would not abandon Adam and Eve to a fate they could not fully understand.

*If the accounts of God's actions in these situations are accurate, they challenge the widespread belief that God was angry with Adam and expelled him from the Garden of Eden purely out of wrath. Instead, the Scriptures consistently portray God as a loving and merciful Creator, whose character remains unchanged throughout time. As Malachi 3:6 (NKJV) affirms, "For I am the Lord, I do not change." This immutable nature of God suggests that His actions toward Adam were not driven by anger but by a deeper purpose rooted in love, justice, mercy, and the overarching plan for redemption.*

## In a Nutshell

## God respected Adam's choice

*The Tree of Life and the Tree of the Knowledge of Good and Evil represent the profound choices given to Adam in the Garden of Eden. The Tree of Life symbolizes the gift of life freely given by God, allowing Adam to enjoy abundant life and unbroken fellowship with his Creator. In contrast, the Tree of the Knowledge of Good and Evil represents a path where life and fellowship with God could only be earned by achieving the righteous standard of God Himself, which is the Law.*

*When Adam and Eve chose to eat from the Tree of the Knowledge of Good and Evil, they effectively opted to pursue God's standards through their own efforts. By doing so, they subjected themselves to the Law, even though they did not yet fully comprehend its requirements. This lack of understanding is evident in the timeline of Scripture, as the explicit Law was given through Moses 2,000 years later to teach humanity the difference between good and evil. Adam's choice was not simply an act of disobedience; it was a covenant, a binding agreement made with God. Because Adam was created in God's image, he bore the responsibility and accountability for his decision, which could not be undone.*

*God, being a covenant-keeping God, honored Adam's free will and the choice he made. To respect this covenant, God removed Adam from the Garden of Eden, ensuring that he would no longer have access to the Tree of Life. This was not an act of punishment but a necessary step to uphold the integrity of the covenant. However, God's nature is not solely one of justice but also of infinite love. Knowing that Adam and his descendants would be unable to achieve righteousness through their own efforts, God had already prepared a plan of redemption. As Revelation 13:8 (NKJV) states, "The Lamb slain from the foundation of the world," God's plan for humanity's salvation through Jesus Christ was established even before creation.*

*This reveals the depth of God's wisdom and love. While respecting Adam's free will and the covenant he entered, God simultaneously made provision for humanity's inability to meet the standard of the Law. Through Jesus Christ, God ensured that the relationship between Him and humanity could be restored, offering redemption and fellowship once again. This highlights the balance between God's justice, His respect for human choice, and His unfailing love and desire to dwell with mankind. It is a testament to His sovereignty and His ultimate plan to reconcile humanity to Himself.*

## Saving the seed

The immeasurable love of God the Father for humanity is evident throughout the Scriptures, as He continually reveals His desire to remain in relationship with mankind. This divine intention is especially clear in His repeated promises to establish the seed of His children across generations. In Psalm 89:4 (NKJV), God declares, "Your seed I will establish forever, and build up your throne to all generations." This statement reflects not only His commitment to the lineage of His chosen people but also His greater plan to ensure that humanity remains connected to Him.

This love is further exemplified in Genesis 3:15 (NKJV), where God speaks directly to the serpent after the fall of mankind, proclaiming, "And I will put enmity between you and the woman, and between your seed and her Seed; He shall bruise your head, and you shall bruise His heel." This declaration goes beyond a curse upon the serpent - it is a profound prophecy of hope. Here, God foretells the coming of Jesus Christ, the promised Seed who would ultimately crush Satan's head and restore what had been lost. This statement demonstrates God's unveiling plan to humanity's fall, His plan of hope to humanity to overcome separation in death and reconcile mankind to Himself.

## Adversary's Plan

Satan, the adversary of God and humanity, was fully aware that his ultimate defeat had been decreed by God. He knew that his fate was sealed, destined to be crushed under the feet of Jesus Christ and His people, as foretold in Genesis 3:15. Despite this certainty, Satan, in his arrogance and rebellion, sought to resist God's plan to bring forth the promised Seed. Knowing his power was limited and his time was short, he devised schemes to corrupt and obstruct the divine lineage through which Christ would come.

One of Satan's most significant efforts to thwart God's plan is described in Genesis 6:2 (NKJV): "The sons of God saw the daughters of men, that they were beautiful; and they took wives for themselves of all whom they chose." This is also found in one of the non-canon manuscripts, Book of Enoch and ancient texts which were found from the Dead Sea scrolls and Ge'ez manuscripts.

In the Book of Enoch (not part of Protestant canon), there is a vivid narrative that portrays Satan and his followers taking an oath to corrupt humanity. This oath, often referred to as the "Oath of the Watchers," is taken by a group of fallen angels, led by a figure named Samyaza, who aligns with Satan's rebellion. Their goal is to defile mankind's lineage and disrupt God's divine plan.

The story unfolds as these angels descend to earth, drawn by their desire for the daughters of men (Enoch 6:1-6). They pledge an oath to act collectively, binding themselves to this rebellious act to ensure none could turn back. They proceed to intermarry with human women, giving rise to the Nephilim, a race of giants known for their violence and corruption (Enoch 7:1-6). This intermingling is depicted as an attempt to corrupt the "seed" of humanity, thwarting God's plan for a chosen lineage through which His purposes would be fulfilled.

As the narrative continues, these fallen beings not only disrupt human genetics but also teach forbidden knowledge to mankind, introducing them to practices such as sorcery, warfare, and other forms of corruption (Enoch 8:1-3). The book emphasizes that their actions contribute to widespread wickedness, as recorded briefly in Genesis 6.

**References**

- *Ge'ez to English Translation: R.H. Charles (1912) is one of the most widely referenced translations of the Book of Enoch from Ge'ez into English.*
- *Dead Sea Scrolls: Published in detailed analyses by scholars like J.T. Milik in The Books of Enoch: Aramaic Fragments of Qumran Cave 4.*

**Divine Plan**

The heart of God was deeply moved with sorrow when He witnessed the corruption of humanity, His creation. This is poignantly described in Genesis 6:5-6 (NKJV): "Then the Lord saw that the wickedness of man was great in the earth, and that every intent of the thoughts of his heart was only evil continually. And the Lord was sorry that He had made man on the earth, and He was grieved in His heart." This grief was not born of anger or wrath toward mankind, but of deep sorrow for what had become of His beloved creation.

Humanity, made in the very image of God, was created to reflect His goodness and enjoy intimate fellowship with Him. However, once mankind became separated from God through transgression, they lost their connection to His wisdom and guidance. This separation left them vulnerable, weak, ignorant of divine ways, and susceptible to the schemes of Satan. No longer walking in harmony with their Creator, mankind became enslaved by sin and driven by the corrupt influence of the enemy.

God chose Noah, one of the pure seeds of Adam, to partner with Him in preserving humanity and His divine plan. As described in Genesis 6:9 (NKJV): "Noah was a just man, perfect in his generations. Noah walked with God." The term "perfect" here is often translated as "blameless," signifying not only Noah's integrity but also the purity of his lineage, untainted by the corruption brought about by the fallen angels. This distinction made Noah the chosen vessel through whom God would preserve the human race and fulfill His covenantal promise.

God entrusted Noah with building the ark, a vessel of salvation. This task was no small endeavor, as it likely took Noah about a century to complete. Genesis 5:32 states that Noah was 500 years old when his sons Shem, Ham, and Japheth were born, and the flood occurred when Noah was 600 years old (Genesis 7:6). During this time, Noah not only labored on the ark but it is also believed he gave warning to his generation of the impending judgment and invited them to turn from their corruption.

In His infinite wisdom and mercy, God preserved Noah and his family, sparing them from the destruction that came upon the earth. Through Noah, God ensured the continuation of the pure seed of Adam, enabling humanity to begin anew and multiply. This act demonstrates God's unwavering love and commitment to His promise to reconcile humanity to Himself.

### In a Nutshell

*The flood that engulfed the entire earth was not an act of anger from God, but rather a decision made with a heavy heart. It was to protect the seed from corruption that had spread throughout humanity, threatening the very purpose of His creation. He carefully preserved the pure seed of His creation through Noah and his family, ensuring that the divine plan to restore the broken relationship with humanity could continue. This act reflects God's unwavering commitment to redemption and His desire to bring humanity back into fellowship with Him.*

## Protecting the Seed

God intervened to save the seed of mankind from being entirely corrupted by the Nephilim, the offspring of fallen angels, ensuring the continuation of His plan for redemption. However, the adversary, Satan, did not cease his efforts. He relentlessly pursued his mission to corrupt the seeds of the earth, attempting to derail God's purpose for humanity. This raises a compelli ng question: Why does God not strip Satan of the power to corrupt mankind?

The answer lies in the unchanging nature of God. As stated in Numbers 23:19 (NLT): “God is not a man, so he does not lie. He is not human, so he does not change his mind.” God’s nature is constant, and His standards are perfect and immutable. What God has given, He does not revoke, even when it comes to Satan. Before his fall, Satan was blessed with power and authority as a created being, and even after his rebellion, God did not retract what He had given. This reflects the extraordinary consistency of God's character and His commitment to His divine principles.

While this leaves mankind vulnerable to Satan’s schemes, it also underscores humanity's dependence on God’s protection and grace. Left to their own devices, humans were frail and powerless before the adversary’s cunning. Therefore, God, in His wisdom, steps in to safeguard the seed of mankind. His intervention ensures that the lineage leading to the promised Savior remains untainted, preserving the pathway for redemption and reconciliation.

## Chosen Generation

The calling of Abram marks a pivotal moment in the biblical narrative, a divine initiative that sets in motion God’s protective plan for the seed of mankind. Abram, later renamed Abraham, is introduced in Genesis 12 as a man living in Ur of the Chaldeans, a city steeped in idolatry. Despite this environment, God called him for a unique and eternal purpose, demonstrating His sovereign ability to call individuals out of obscurity into covenantal relationships.

This call requires Abram to leave everything familiar, his homeland, his relatives, and his father's household. It is a call to trust God completely, to step into the unknown with nothing but the promise of divine guidance and blessing. The promise itself is extraordinary: God pledges to make Abram the father of a great nation, to bless him, and to extend that blessing to all the families of the earth through him. It is a covenant rooted in grace, underscoring God's intention to use Abram's response as a vehicle for worldwide redemption.

The purpose behind God's calling of Abraham was far greater than just blessing one man or one generation, it was the beginning of a divine plan to raise a nation, Israel, through which Jesus Christ, the Savior of the world, would come. This foundational calling sets the stage for the unfolding narrative of redemption. However, one question has persisted throughout history: Why Israel? Why were they chosen to be the special people of God?

The answer lies in the faith of Abraham, who believed in God and responded to His call with unwavering trust. When God spoke, Abraham made the bold decision to step out and chose to walk into the unknown, trusting solely in the promises of a God he could not see but whose voice he knew was true. Had Abraham chosen not to obey, the narrative could have been different. God's purposes are not dependent on any one individual. If

Abraham had hesitated or refused, God would have called another, and the pages of Scripture would have recorded the name of the one who chose to believe and partner with Him. But it was Abraham who responded in faith, and it is his name that stands as a keystone in the history of redemption.

**Building a tower**

When humanity, through Abraham, entered into a covenantal partnership with God, He began to establish a divine safeguard around His chosen people. This protection is beautifully symbolized in Proverbs 18:10 (NKJV): "The name of the Lord is a strong tower; the righteous run to it and are safe." This "tower" was not merely a physical separation but a boundary that sanctified His people, setting them apart from the world to preserve the lineage through which His ultimate redemptive plan would unfold.

To mark this covenant, God instituted the practice of circumcision, a physical sign that carried profound spiritual meaning. By removing the male foreskin, the very place through which the seed of the next generation would pass, God emphasized the sanctity of the lineage. This is explicitly stated in Genesis 17:14 (NKJV): "And the uncircumcised male child, who is not circumcised in the flesh of his foreskin, that person shall be cut off from his people; he has broken My covenant." Circumcision was more than a ritual, it was a sacred reminder of God's promise and the role of Abraham's descendants in carrying His divine purpose until Jesus Christ, "the Seed" that is promised in Genesis 3.

God also commanded the Israelites to refrain from intermarrying with other nations, as seen in Deuteronomy 7:3-4 (NKJV): "Nor shall you make marriages with them. You shall not give your daughter to their son, nor take their daughter for your son. For they will turn your sons away from following Me" This directive was not about exclusion but preservation. By keeping Israel distinct from the seed being corrupted, God was protecting the chosen lineage through which Jesus, the promised Messiah, would come.

The strict consequences for breaking these commands were not rooted in God's anger but in His deep desire to maintain the sanctity of the covenant and ensure the fulfillment of His redemptive plan. God's ultimate goal was to bring forth Jesus Christ, the Seed through whom humanity would be reconciled to Him. This protective boundary was an act of love and purpose, designed to preserve the path for salvation and restore the broken relationship between God and mankind.

### In a Nutshell

*Father God, in His divine wisdom, set Israel apart as a chosen nation, placing a protective boundary around them to safeguard His covenant and preserve the purity of the seed. This separation ensured that Israel would remain distinct, free from the corrupting influences of the fallen angels and the surrounding nations. By isolating them, God created a spiritual and physical sanctuary where His redemptive plan could unfold, shielding His chosen people from external threats while preparing the lineage through which His promises would be fulfilled.*

## Learn to See and Obey

The moment Adam and Eve reached out and ate from the Tree of the Knowledge of Good and Evil, they entered a new reality, one defined by the law of good and evil, a divine standard that now governed their existence. Their once-innocent state was transformed as they came under the expectation to be aware of moral distinctions and accountability. However, despite stepping into this realm, they were not yet fully bound to the law. Their understanding was immature, like that of infants stepping into a world, they could not yet comprehend.

In this sense, Adam and Eve were like newborns to the covenant of the law. They had crossed a threshold, but their awareness of the full weight of their actions and the demands of the law was incomplete. Much like a child learning to navigate life's complexities, they lacked the maturity and insight required to fully grasp the divine framework into which they had entered. God, in His infinite wisdom and mercy, responded to their actions with both justice and compassion. Though they were held accountable, He recognized their inability to fully comprehend what they had done.

### New Born

A newborn baby is so delicate and utterly dependent, it is one of the most precious gifts life can offer. Their fragility and innocence embody a purity that is unmatched, evoking a deep sense of wonder in all who behold them. From their very first breath, they capture the hearts of those around them, stirring an awe that transcends words. These tiny beings, unable to feed themselves, clean themselves, or even articulate their needs, teach us profound lessons about the sanctity of life and the privilege of care.

This vividly portrays the state of humanity in Adam after being sent out of the Garden of Eden. They were utterly dependent on God, unable even to grasp the depth of His laws or comprehend the requirements of obedience. In God's eyes, they were fragile, precious, and innocent like newborns breathing their first in the realm of the law. Although their disobedience had consequences, their state was one of spiritual infancy, requiring guidance and nurturing.

God, in His infinite compassion, treated humanity as a loving parent would care for an infant. Just as a caregiver patiently cleans a baby who has soiled themselves, God repeatedly forgave and cleansed His people when they transgressed. Recognizing their inability to fully understand or adhere to His ways, He offered them the pure milk of obedience, nurturing their growth step by step. They were not yet ready for the solid food of deeper spiritual truths and responsibilities. This idea is echoed in Paul's words in 1 Corinthians 3:1-2 (NKJV): "And I, brethren, could not speak to you as to spiritual people but as to carnal, as to babes in Christ. I fed you with milk and not with solid food; for until now you were not able to receive it."

**Weaned**

When a child is born, their entire existence depends on their caregivers. Milk, the first nourishment of life, sustains their fragile body, offering comfort and security. This phase of infancy is marked by absolute dependence on the mother. However, as the child grows stronger and their needs evolve, a natural transition begins, the process of weaning. Weaning is not just about physical nourishment; it is about equipping the child to engage with the world in new ways. It is a gradual separation, as the child begins to rely less on milk and more on solid food to sustain their growth.

In Jewish culture, the weaning of a child was not just a practical milestone but a deeply significant event, often marked with celebration and gratitude. It symbolized a pivotal transition in the child's development, a moment of growth and independence that carried spiritual and familial meaning. The story of Isaac's weaning in Genesis 21:8 underscores its importance: "So the child grew and was weaned. And Abraham made a great feast on the same day that Isaac was weaned." For Abraham, this event was more than a personal family milestone; it was an opportunity to honor God's faithfulness in Isaac's growth and survival through the vulnerable years of infancy.

The significance of weaning as a moment of transition is further emphasized in the story of Hannah, as recorded in 1 Samuel 1:22 (NKJV): "Not until the child is weaned; then I will take him, that he may appear before the Lord and remain there forever." This reflects Hannah's commitment to dedicating her son, Samuel, to the service of the Lord. In this context, weaning represented a stage of independence from the mother, signifying that the child was ready to begin a new phase of life and, in Samuel's case, his lifelong ministry in God's house. Weaning, therefore, was seen as a profound shift not only in the physical nourishment of the child but also in their readiness to step into new roles and responsibilities.

**In a Nutshell**

*In the case of humanity, through Adam, mankind was not fully bound to the law until it was given through Moses at Mount Sinai. Moreover, the law was presented only after the people declared their willingness to obey, as recorded in Exodus 19:8 (NLT): "We will do everything the Lord has commanded." In the very next chapter, Exodus 20, the Ten Commandments were delivered, marking the formal introduction of the law. This moment represents the spiritual weaning of humanity, transitioning from a state of dependency to accepting the solid food of the law, just as a child moves from milk to solid food when ready to handle greater responsibility, humanity was stepping into a new phase, embracing the challenge of obedience - unaware that it was a standard they would ultimately never be able to attain, symbolizing their beginning into covenant of law with God which they chose in Adam by eating from the Tree of Knowledge of Good and Evil.*

## Opportunity to prove

The law, referred to as the Torah for Israelites, holds a central and sacred role in religious, ethical, and communal life. The law is far more than a legal code; it is a living, breathing testament to their relationship with God. It is a treasure that brings purpose, guidance, and meaning to their lives. By observing the law, they express their faith, gratitude, and devotion, striving to live in harmony with God's will. To Jews, the Torah is not just a guide for life, it is the heart of faith, a bridge between the divine and humanity, and the foundation of their enduring covenant with God.

Israelites treated the law with the utmost reverence. It was read, studied, and memorized diligently. In synagogues, the Torah scrolls are housed in an ark (Aron Kodesh) and are treated with great honor. When read publicly, the congregation rises, and the scrolls are adorned with decorative coverings, emphasizing their sanctity. Daily life was meticulously shaped by the law. From dietary practices (Kashrut) to Sabbath observance, every detail of Jewish life was informed by the Torah. These practices were not seen as restrictive but as ways to sanctify daily activities and bring God's presence into every aspect of life.

However, as the pages of history unfold, it becomes evident that this reverence, though sincere, often failed to translate into consistent obedience. Time and again, the Israelites struggled to live up to the standards of the law, faltering in their faithfulness to God. The golden calf incident at the base of Mount Sinai itself (Exodus 32), mere weeks after receiving the commandments, became a tragic testament to human frailty and disobedience.

### Judges

In times when Israel turned away from God, falling into idolatry and rebellion, their disobedience often led to foreign oppression. Yet, in their distress, when they cried out for deliverance, God responded by appointing judges, leaders equipped with divine authority and wisdom to restore order and bring His people back to the covenant. These judges were not kings or rulers, but individuals chosen by God to act as instruments of deliverance for Israel.

Judges like Deborah, Gideon, and Samson stand as powerful examples of how God works through flawed but faithful individuals to achieve His purposes. Deborah, a prophetess and the only female judge recorded in the scriptures, demonstrated remarkable courage and leadership, guiding Israel to victory over their oppressors while reminding them of their covenant with God. Gideon, though initially hesitant and doubtful, became a mighty warrior for the Lord, delivering Israel with a small but divinely empowered army, showing that victory belongs to God, not human strength. Samson, despite his personal failings, was used by God to confront Israel’s enemies and begin the process of liberation.

The accounts recorded in scripture emphasize the recurring theme of the Israelites' inability to uphold the law and the consistent display of God’s mercy and intervention during periods of chaos and despair. Each judge, in their own distinct way, exemplifies God's capacity to work through flawed individuals to fulfill His perfect will. Through their triumphs and struggles, the narrative reveals the unwavering truth that God remains faithful to His promises, persistently calling His people back to Him, regardless of how far they have drifted.

**Kings**

God, in His boundless mercy, provided the Israelites with a king when they rejected Him as their King, as described in 1 Samuel 8:7 (NIV): "The Lord told him: 'Listen to all that the people are saying to you; it is not you they have rejected, but they have rejected me as their king.'" This pivotal moment marked a transition in Israel's history, as the people, yearning to be like the nations around them, chose earthly leadership over divine sovereignty.

Among the kings of Israel, there were those like David, a man after God's own heart, and Josiah, who remained faithful to the Lord throughout their lives, exemplifying steadfast devotion and righteous leadership. These kings served as shining examples of how God could use human leaders to guide His people back to Him. Yet, not all kings upheld the same faithfulness. Many rulers strayed from God's commandments, leading the nation into idolatry, corruption, and spiritual decline.

Despite the influence of righteous or wicked kings, the Israelites repeatedly struggled to obey the laws given to them at Mount Sinai. Their covenant with God, though sacred, was continuously broken as the people faltered in their commitment to live according to His will. This cycle of disobedience underscores the limitations of human leadership and the persistent nature of their need for God.

**Prophets**

Throughout the Old Testament, the voices of the prophets resonate as beacons of divine truth, delivering God's messages of warning, hope, and redemption. These chosen messengers stood as intermediaries between God and His people, calling Israel back to the covenant and urging them to abandon their sinful ways. Prophets such as Isaiah, Jeremiah, and Ezekiel carried the weight of their divine commission with unwavering dedication, confronting the spiritual and moral corruption of their time.

Isaiah, known for his profound visions, reminded the people of God's holiness and His plan for redemption, often prophesying about the coming of the Messiah who would restore all things. Jeremiah, often referred to as the weeping prophet, boldly confronted the persistent idolatry and rebellion of Israel, warning of the consequences of their disobedience while offering the hope of a renewed covenant. Ezekiel, through vivid and often symbolic imagery, spoke of cleansing the land and the people, emphasizing God's desire to restore His sanctuary among them and renew their hearts.

These prophets did not merely convey messages; they embodied God's relentless pursuit of His people. Their words served as both a mirror, reflecting Israel's failures, and a light, illuminating the path back to righteousness. Through their proclamations, they reminded Israel of God's unchanging promises, promises rooted in His covenantal love and faithfulness.

### In a Nutshell

*Through the periods of the Judges, Kings, and Prophets, the Israelites consistently struggled to maintain the deep and sweet fellowship with God for which they were originally created. God had intended humanity to live in communion with Him, but the choice of their covenant, represented by the Tree of the Knowledge of Good and Evil, placed them under the weight of the law. This path, though chosen by mankind, in Adam, revealed humanity's inability to fully uphold the covenant's demands.*

*Jesus Himself highlighted this failure in John 5:45 (NKJV) when He said, "There is one who accuses you, Moses, in whom you trust." This statement reflects how the law, symbolizing the knowledge of good and evil, became a standard that humanity could not meet, ultimately exposing their shortcomings. The Israelites, trusting in the law given through Moses, found themselves accused by the very covenant they relied upon. Instead of achieving the fellowship with God that was intended, the law illuminated their dependence on God's mercy and their need for a greater redemptive solution.*

## God's summary of mankind failure

The book of Malachi, divinely recorded as the 39th and final book of the Old Testament, stands as a poignant conclusion to the sacred writings before the opening of the New Testament with the Gospel of Matthew. Every word in this book is orchestrated by the Holy Spirit, weaving together a profound summary of the Old Testament's overarching narrative.

Within its pages, the book captures the persistent struggles of mankind, highlighting the corruption of the priesthood, the betrayal of God's trust through infidelity, and the nation's spiritual complacency. It reveals God's heartbreak over their unfaithfulness, yet also His relentless desire to restore the relationship. Malachi does not stop at recounting failures; it points forward with hope, prophesying the coming of God's Son, the Messiah, pointing to Jesus Christ, who would bring redemption and renewal.

The book culminates in the promise of the "Great Day of the Lord," a Day of Judgment and restoration, where the Messiah would establish righteousness and reconcile humanity to God. As the final voice of the Old Testament, Malachi bridges the gap between the covenants, humanity's inability and ultimate need for God to restore their relationship.

**Malachi 1**

"Malachi 1 opens with a declaration of God's enduring love for Israel, a love that the people fail to recognize or appreciate as said in Malachi 1:2 (NKJV) "I have loved you," says the Lord.

"Yet you say, 'In what way have You loved us?" Despite questioning His care, God reminds them of His covenantal faithfulness, contrasting His choice of Jacob with His rejection of Esau to demonstrate His unwavering commitment. However, the chapter shifts to reveal the spiritual decline of Israel, particularly through the actions of the priests and the people. They offer defiled sacrifices - blemished and inferior animals - on God's altar, showing contempt for His holiness. God confronts their dishonor, likening their irreverence to a servant disrespecting a master or a son disobeying a father. Malachi 1:6 (NKJV) says "A son honors his father." He warns that insincere worship cannot please Him and declares that His name will be glorified among the nations, even if His own people fail to honor Him. The chapter concludes with a solemn reminder of God's greatness as the King of all creation, calling His people to return to a genuine reverence for Him."

**Malachi 2**

Malachi 2 continues God's rebuke of Israel, focusing on the unfaithfulness of the priests and the people. The chapter begins with a stern warning to the priests who have dishonored God's name through their corrupt practices and failure to teach His laws. The chapter then turns to address the people's betrayal in their relationships, particularly their unfaithfulness in marriage. God condemns their practice of divorcing their wives and marrying foreign women who worship other gods, calling it a betrayal of the covenant community. He emphasizes that marriage is a sacred union designed to produce godly offspring and reminds them that He hates divorce because it undermines the sanctity of this bond.

**Malachi 3**

The chapter opens with the promise of a messenger who will prepare the way for the Lord, heralding a future day of divine intervention. God declares that He will come swiftly to His temple, bringing with Him both purification and judgment. He will refine the priests like gold and silver, restoring their ability to present sacrifices that are pleasing in His sight. The chapter concludes with a powerful affirmation from God, highlighting the importance of the "book of remembrance." This sacred record is written to honor those who fear Him and meditate on His name, serving as a testament to their devotion and faithfulness. In a moment of reassurance, God proclaims, “They shall be Mine.” This declaration reflects His unchanging love and faithfulness to those who revere Him, marking them as His cherished possession and promising His protection and favor in the days to come.

**Malachi 4**

This chapter presents a prophetic vision of the coming of the Lord, emphasizing both the hope and the awe that His arrival will bring. In Malachi 4:2 (NKJV), the imagery of “The Sun of Righteousness shall arise, with healing in His wings” points unmistakably to Jesus Christ. It speaks of His mission to bring healing and restoration to a broken humanity, offering redemption to those who had miserably failed to uphold the covenant.

The chapter also addresses the "dreadful day of the Lord," a multifaceted prophecy that encompasses both His first coming and His ultimate return. It alludes to

Jesus' earthly ministry, His sacrificial death, and His resurrection, which set the stage for a profound transformation in humanity's relationship with God. This redemptive work is further highlighted in Malachi 4:6 (NKJV): "And he will turn the hearts of the fathers to the children, and the hearts of the children to their fathers." This verse symbolizes the reconciliation that Christ's coming would initiate—not only between people but also between humanity and the heavenly Father.

The chapter weaves together themes of judgment as hope, and restoration, offering a glimpse into God's plan to heal the rift between Himself and His people. It portrays the coming of the Messiah as both a fulfillment of divine justice and an act of unparalleled mercy, turning the hearts of His children back to their Creator and restoring the unity that had been lost.

### In a Nutshell

*The book of Malachi, the final book of the Old Testament, serves as a divine summary of humanity's spiritual state and the need for Jesus Christ. It highlights mankind's repeated failures and inability to earn fellowship with God through their own efforts.*

*Malachi critiques human disobedience while pointing to the coming of the Messiah as the ultimate solution to restore the broken relationship, bridging the Old and New Testaments with a message of hope and redemption.*

## Fulfillment of all Laws

Throughout the ages, the spiritual state of humanity has been marked by a struggle to maintain fellowship with God. From the earliest days, even before the giving of the law, from Adam to Moses, mankind wandered aimlessly, like lost sheep without a shepherd, unable to grasp the depth of God's heart or His intentions for them. Despite their inherent longing for purpose and relationship with their Creator, they lacked the means to bridge the gap created by their choice.

When the law was given at Mount Sinai, it offered humanity a divine standard, a way to live in alignment with God's will. Yet, from the moment of its introduction until the coming of Jesus Christ, mankind continually fell short of its demands. While they strove to keep the law, their efforts were insufficient, revealing their inability to achieve true fellowship with God. Many clung to the belief that they understood and fulfilled the law, measuring themselves by their own standards. However, their actions and hearts fell short of the truth: they failed not just in practice but in understanding the spirit of the law itself.

This recurring failure underscores humanity's need for something greater, a Savior who could fulfill the law perfectly and restore the broken relationship between God and mankind. It reveals a central theme of Scripture: that human effort alone is insufficient to achieve reconciliation with God, and only through divine grace can the taste of true fellowship be realized.

**Why Jesus?**

The covenant established through the Tree of the Knowledge of Good and Evil was initiated by Adam, marking a defining moment that bound humanity to the consequences of that choice. Similar to a marriage, a covenant signifies a binding relationship, one that remains intact until dissolved by the death of one party. As described in Romans 7:2 (NKJV), "For the woman who has a husband is bound by the law to her husband as long as he lives. But if the husband dies, she is released from the law of her husband."

In this context, God's law embodies His perfect and immutable standard, which, by its very nature, cannot cease to exist or "die." This creates a significant dilemma: if the law remains unchanging, the only way to sever the covenant formed through Adam is through the death of humanity itself. Such a resolution, however, would contradict God's purpose in creating humanity - to live in fellowship with Him and reflect His glory.

The only viable alternative is for someone to fulfill the requirements of the law perfectly, addressing God's standard while bridging the separation caused by Adam's transgression. Without such fulfillment, humanity faces eternal separation from God, a spiritual death. This covenant, with all its profound implications, set the stage for the redemptive mission of Jesus Christ, who is referred to as the "last Adam" in 1 Corinthians 15:45 (NKJV): "The last Adam became a life-giving spirit." This title underscores His divine purpose - to reverse the separation between humanity and God caused by the first Adam's failure.

Jesus, the only begotten Son of God within the triune Godhead, willingly relinquished His divine privileges and took on the form of humanity. Philippians 2:5-7 (NKJV) vividly describes this selfless act: “Let this mind be in you which was also in Christ Jesus, who, being in the form of God, did not consider it robbery to be equal with God, but made Himself of no reputation, taking the form of a bondservant, and coming in the likeness of men.”

Although equal with God in His divine nature, Jesus did not cling to His heavenly glory at the expense of humanity’s redemption. Instead, He humbled Himself entirely, entering into the frailty of human existence. By assuming human flesh, He subjected Himself to the very conditions and limitations faced by humanity, aligning Himself with the covenant of the law that Adam had failed to uphold.

This act was essential because only a human, bound by the same covenant, could fulfill the law’s demands. The divine covenant required that humanity's failure be addressed by humanity itself. However, no descendant of Adam was capable of meeting the law’s perfect standard. Thus, Jesus came as the perfect man, fully human, to fulfill the covenant in its entirety. His mission was the ultimate expression of divine love and justice, bridging the separation between humanity and God.

**What did Jesus do?**

The Bible explicitly affirms that Jesus died for humanity, as stated in Romans 5:8 (NKJV): "But God demonstrates His own love toward us, in that while we were still sinners, Christ died for us." This verse highlights the depth of God's love, as Jesus willingly gave His life for the redemption of humanity. However, Jesus' death holds an even greater significance, it was not only for humanity but also as humanity, its essence is reflected in Colossians 3:3 (NKJV): "For you died, and your life is hidden with Christ in God."

*Our death was hidden in Adam, leaving humanity unable to be reconciled to the Father. Now, through the last Adam, Jesus Christ, our life is securely hidden in Him, and can never be separated from the Father. Work of Jesus Christ in binding us to the Father is Stronger the Work of Adam separating from Him.*

**Walking**

Jesus, during His time on earth, was fully human, experiencing the realities of humanity. Yet, even as a man, He embodied a life of miraculous power. He raised the dead, healed the sick, walked on water, calmed raging storms, fed thousands with little, and ultimately conquered death itself. These extraordinary acts, however, were not performed solely because He was God, for if His miracles stemmed only from His divine nature, the very foundation of salvation would be undermined. The covenant with God required fulfillment by a man, not through divine exemption but through human obedience and reliance on the Father.

Through His life and actions, Jesus left this legacy, demonstrating the potential of humanity when fully aligned with God. This legacy points to a reality described in Romans 8:19-21 (NKJV): "For the earnest expectation of the creation eagerly waits for the revealing of the sons of God. For the creation was subjected to futility, not willingly, but because of Him who subjected it in hope; because the creation itself also will be delivered from the bondage of corruption into the glorious liberty of the children of God."

This passage speaks of the day when humanity, as the sons and daughters of God, will be revealed in their full glory. In that moment, the liberty and power Jesus walked in on earth will be mirrored in His followers. It is a vision of humanity restored to its intended purpose, free from corruption and walking in the same authority, grace, and fellowship with the Father as Jesus demonstrated. This is not just a hope for the future after physical death and resurrection but a calling to live in alignment with that promise now, reflecting the transformative power of being children of God.

**Seeing**

In addition to leaving a legacy that demonstrated how humanity could walk on this earth in alignment with God's will, Jesus also introduced a transformative understanding of God's nature. He revealed God not merely as a distant Creator or a sovereign Judge but as a loving Father. This profound perspective reshaped humanity's relationship with God, fostering intimacy, trust, and a sense of belonging.

This shift is beautifully illustrated in the Gospel of Luke 11:2 (NKJV), where Jesus teaches His disciples how to pray, saying, “When you pray, say: ‘Our Father in heaven.’” With these words, Jesus invited mankind to approach God with the confidence of a child addressing a father, emphasizing a personal and familial relationship rather than one based solely on formality or fear.

By referring to God as "Father," Jesus bridged the gap between humanity and the divine, offering a new lens through which to understand God’s love, care, and provision. This teaching not only redefined prayer but also instilled in humanity the assurance that they are children of a heavenly Father who desires a deep and enduring relationship with them. It was a revelation that invited all people to see themselves as part of God’s family, united in love and purpose under His fatherly care.

**In a Nutshell**

*In the Gospel of Matthew 5:17 (NKJV), Jesus stated, “Do not think that I came to destroy the Law or the Prophets. I did not come to destroy but to fulfill.” This fulfillment not only includes redeeming humanity from death but also showing the way to walk as HE walk ed on this earth and how to see the almighty God as a loving Father as He sees.*

## Your will be done

The eternal purpose of God in creating Adam was rooted in His desire for fellowship, a deep, abiding relationship within the divine family. Adam was crafted by God's own hands, a being uniquely formed to reflect His image and invited into the triune family of the Father, much like a newborn child is welcomed into a loving home. God's intention was not merely to create a being to inhabit the earth but to share a bond of mutual love and communion that would last forever.

In this perfect relationship, God endowed Adam with dominion over the earth, granting him the authority to rule and steward creation as an extension of God's own sovereignty. This dominion was not only a responsibility but also a privilege, symbolizing Adam's role as a beloved son entrusted with his Father's creation. In this sacred design, God sought to love Adam and to be loved by him, forming an eternal bond of intimacy, and joy.

### Adam was not created to die

When God formed Adam from the dust of the ground and breathed into his nostrils the breath of life, bringing him into existence, His intention was not for Adam to return to the ground from which he was made. Instead, God's purpose was to share an eternal fellowship with Adam, a relationship rooted in love, harmony, and unbroken communion.

This tragic return to dust is reflected in Genesis 3:19 (NKJV): "For dust you are, and to dust you shall return." These words, spoken by God after Adam's transgression, signify the spiritual and physical mortality that became mankind's destiny because of his choice. Adam, who was created to reflect God's image and live in His presence forever, was now subject to the limitations of the flesh and the finality of returning to dust.

This divine purpose was not limited to Adam as an individual but extended to all of humanity in Adam. The blessing of God on Adam, even before the fall, reveals His broader plan for mankind. In Genesis 1:22 (NKJV), it is written, "And God blessed them, saying, 'Be fruitful and multiply, and fill the waters in the seas, and let birds multiply on the earth.'" This blessing signified God's intention for all humanity to thrive, flourish, and steward His creation in harmony with His will.

Had Adam not chosen to eat from the Tree of the Knowledge of Good and Evil, the trajectory of human history would have been vastly different. Death, with all its byproducts such as sickness, pain, and sorrow, would never have entered the world. Humanity would have continued to live in a state of perfect harmony, enjoying uninterrupted fellowship with God on earth.

## Curse Reversed

The Scriptures provide a compelling connection between Jesus Christ and the Ark of Noah, as seen in 1 Peter 3:20-21 (NKJV): "When once the Divine longsuffering waited in the days of Noah, while the ark was being prepared, in which a few, that is, eight souls, were saved through water. There is also an antitype which now saves us, "baptism" through the resurrection of Jesus

Christ." This passage draws a parallel between entering the ark and entering into Jesus Christ.

The narrative of Noah, as recorded in Genesis 8:4 (NKJV), further enriches this symbolism: "Then the ark rested in the seventh month, the seventeenth day of the month, on the mountains of Ararat." The word "Ararat" holds significant meaning, as it translates to "the curse is reversed." This detail points to Jesus' redemptive work, as He not only provides salvation but also reverses the curse of sin and death.

As Paul writes in Galatians 3:13 (NKJV): "Christ has redeemed us from the curse of the law." Through His death and resurrection, Jesus has freed humanity from sin and death. His redemptive work goes beyond lifting the curse; it positions believers in a place where the curse is reversed, allowing them to experience restoration and renewed fellowship with the Father.

**Kingdom**

A Kingdom is defined by several key elements that collectively shape its identity and function. At the heart of a kingdom is its sovereign, the king, who serves as the central figure of authority and symbolizes unity and power. The king's rule extends over a defined territory, the domain of the kingdom, marked by its boundaries. Within this realm are the people, the subjects who owe their allegiance to the king and form the social and cultural fabric of the kingdom. The governance of the kingdom is maintained through a structured system of laws and customs, often administered by appointed officials to ensure order and the execution of the king's will. Beyond this framework, a kingdom also embodies a rich cultural identity, reflecting the shared traditions, language, and history of its people. These elements come together to create a realm of authority and belonging, where leadership, territory, and community are unified under the banner of its King.

Children of God are called to be both kings and priests in God's Kingdom, a role that reflects authority. This divine calling is rooted in God's original design for humanity and fulfilled through Jesus Christ. In Revelation 1:5-6 (NKJV), it is declared, "To Him who loved us and washed us from our sins in His own blood, and has made us kings and priests to His God and Father, to Him be glory and dominion forever and ever."

As king and priests in His kingdom, children of God are given the authority in Christ to reign in life. This does not limit to earthly domination but also to spiritual authority over sin, death, and the powers of darkness. It is the restoration of humanity's original mandate, as seen in Genesis 1:28, where God gave Adam and Eve dominion over creation. Through Jesus, the last Adam, this royal authority is reclaimed, allowing believers to walk in victory and represent God's Kingdom on earth.

Is the Kingdom of God meant only for the afterlife? Absolutely not. The will of the Father is clearly revealed when Jesus taught His disciples to pray in Matthew 6:9-10 (NKJV): "Our Father in heaven, Hallowed be Your name. Your kingdom come. Your will be done On earth as it is in heaven." This prayer emphasizes that God's desire is not for humanity to simply die and return to Him, but for mankind to live in communion with Him on earth, reflecting His Kingdom and fulfilling His will here and now.

### In a Nutshell

*The heart of the Father is to dwell within us, not merely for us to die and return to Him. This is beautifully expressed in John 14:23 (NKJV), where Jesus said, "If anyone loves Me, he will keep My word; and My Father will love him, and We will come to him and make Our home with him." God's ultimate desire is to establish His presence within us, creating a living relationship where He resides in the hearts of those who love Him.*

### Answers to ponder

The Bible presents an incredible storyline, depicting the journey of humanity and outlining mankind's repeated failures in their choices. However, these failures do not diminish the unwavering love of the Father for humanity. God's determination to bring us into His family remains steadfast, no matter the cost, even to the extent of Jesus giving up His Godhead, taking the form of mankind just because mankind, in Adam, chose to earn the fellowship by keeping the law. He loves us and respects our choice and fulfills His purpose in our choice, no matter what!

## Summary - Bible Journey

Many times, the narrative we create about the Bible portrays God the Father as an angry and wrathful figure - one who was furious with Adam, destroyed humanity in the flood, and punished people whenever they sinned and His response to mankind depends on their actions.

Yet, paradoxically, this same God is said to have loved humanity so much that He gave His only begotten Son, Jesus, to save us from sin. Such an interpretation can lead to a distorted view of God's character.

To truly grasp the message of the Bible, it is essential to read it in context and view it through the lens of Jesus Christ, who reveals the heart of the Father. When seen in this light, it becomes clear that the Father is consistent and unchanging, displaying the same love and mercy in both the Old and New Testaments. He is not a punishing God in the Old Testament who suddenly transforms into a loving Father in the New Testament, nor is His anger "satisfied" through Jesus as though it defines His nature. Instead, the truth is that God has always been a loving Father, steadfast in His grace and mercy, guiding humanity through His unchanging character of love.

The storyline of the Bible reflects His continual effort to reconcile with humanity, demonstrating both justice and compassion as expressions of the same divine love. Jesus does not change the Father's nature; He reveals it fully, showing that the Father's love has been constant throughout all of history.

**Take Away**

When one begins to comprehend the grand narrative of the Bible, the heart of the Father, and the work of Jesus Christ, a profound transformation occurs. It opens the door to living in alignment with God's divine purpose, allowing His will to manifest on earth as it is in heaven. Understanding the Father's deep love and unwavering commitment to humanity, combined with the sacrificial and restorative work of Jesus, empowers humanity to embody the Kingdom of God in their daily lives.

Through this revelation, individuals can act as vessels of God's presence, bringing peace, love, and joy wherever they go. It is not just about waiting for a future heavenly reward but actively participating in the fulfillment of God's plan here and now. By walking in this understanding, believers carry the essence of heaven, its values, its love, and its power, into their earthly existence, creating a tangible reflection of God's Kingdom on earth.

## My Reflection

*I was born into a Hindu family in India, but from a very young age, I felt a deep yearning for the love of God. That search led me to accept Jesus Christ at the age of 14, and I was baptized in water. This decision was not an easy one, as my mother was strictly against me embracing Christianity. My two elder sisters and I chose to keep our baptisms a secret, knowing the consequences if she found out.*

*When I was in 11th grade (junior year), my sister was attending college, and I discovered that she was part of a university students' fellowship. It was a secret gathering for believing students, where they could worship, have fellowship, and partake in communion. I had never taken communion since my baptism, and hearing about this stirred a deep desire within me. I longed to be part of that fellowship, but I had no idea how to find the place.*

*One day, after school, I decided to try. I knew the fellowship was located around two or three k kilometers from a church, so I took a public bus to the church, praying silently that I would find my way.*

*Time was tight-I needed to be home before my mother returned from work. Standing in front of the church, I prayed, asking the Lord to guide me so I could finally take part in communion. With no address or directions, I began to walk, speaking to the Holy Spirit and trusting His guidance. Whenever I felt lost or unsure of which way to go, I heard a small, still voice giving me directions.*

*Eventually, I found myself near a cemetery across from several houses. I felt the Holy Spirit prompting me to knock on one of the doors. Fear crept in - I didn't know who lived there, and by then, it was getting dark. On top of that, I had no idea how to find my way back home if things went wrong. I stood there for a while, frozen with uncertainty. Finally, I mustered the courage to obey the Holy Spirit and knocked on the door.*

*To my absolute surprise, the person who opened the door was my sister! We were all shocked and overwhelmed by the way God had guided me to that very spot. That evening, I experienced an amazing time of fellowship and took part in communion for the first time since my baptism. It was a moment of spiritual joy and renewal that I will never forget.*

*This experience taught me the importance of walking in obedience to the Holy Spirit. Sometimes, it takes courage to step out in faith, especially when the path ahead is unclear. But when we listen to Him and take that first step, He leads us in ways we cannot imagine, aligning us with His purpose. That day, I realized that walking with the Holy Spirit means walking as Jesus did - trusting completely, even in the unknown.*

# Chapter - 4
# LAW

## Introduction

In general view, a law serves as a structured set of rules established by a recognized authority to guide behavior and maintain order within a community or society. These rules are created with the intention of promoting fairness, resolving conflicts, and safeguarding the rights of individuals while also outlining consequences for those who fail to adhere to them. Laws are typically documented in official records, such as constitutions, legal codes, or statutes, and their enforcement is carried out by designated institutions. By providing a framework for accountability and justice, laws aim to foster a stable and harmonious environment where societal values are upheld and disputes can be addressed in an organized manner.

Jewish tradition is deeply rooted in a rich collection of sacred texts, each serving a unique purpose in guiding religious, ethical, and daily life. Central to these texts is the Tanakh, which encompasses the foundational writings of Judaism, including the narratives of the prophets, hymns of devotion, poetic songs, and timeless wisdom literature. Complementing this is the Mishnah, a compilation of rabbinic teachings and legal discourse that forms the cornerstone of Jewish oral law. Expanding upon the Mishnah is the Talmud, a monumental work of commentary and debate, exploring questions of law, ethics, and philosophy through the insights of generations of scholars. The Midrash offers another layer of interpretation, weaving together allegorical stories, parables, and legal insights to illuminate the deeper meanings of the scriptures. Halakhah, a body of legal literature, provides detailed guidance on every aspect of Jewish living, from ritual observances to ethical conduct. At the heart of it all lies the

Torah, revered as the divinely revealed law given to Moses during the Exodus, serving as both a spiritual and legal foundation for the Jewish faith. Together, these texts form an interconnected framework that has shaped Jewish thought and practice for millennia.

This chapter embarks on an exploration of the mysteries embedded within the law, uncovering its deeper meanings and implications. It begins with an examination of the Torah, the cornerstone of divine law, seeking to understand its purpose and the wisdom it conveys. Attention then turns to Moses, who stands as the quintessential figure embodying the law, representing its authority and the covenant it establishes. The discussion further delves into the inherent limitations and capabilities of the law, clarifying what it is designed to accomplish and where its boundaries lie. Central to this exploration is the divine intent behind the giving of the law, its role in humanity, fostering relationship with God, and to shape moral conduct. Finally, the chapter reflects on how the law is represented to humanity in the person of Jesus Christ. Together, these elements weave a rich tapestry of understanding that reveals the enduring relevance and spiritual depth of the law.

**Questions to ponder**

- What is Law
- Why was the law given to mankind

## Torah

The Torah holds a place of utmost significance in the Jewish faith, revered as the foundational law book and containing the first five books of the Hebrew Bible: Genesis, Exodus, Leviticus, Numbers, and Deuteronomy. The term "Torah" (תּוֹרָה), as identified in Hebrew Strong's Concordance #8451, carries a profound meaning, encompassing law, instruction, and teaching.

Derived from the root word "yarah" (יָרָה), it evokes imagery of flowing water, symbolizing nourishment, clarity, and direction. This root word also conveys the act of pointing out, guiding, and teaching, which underscores the purpose of Torah.

The question arises: what does the Torah aim to teach or instruct? Jesus provides an illuminating answer in the Gospel of John 5:39 (NLT), where he declares, "You search the Scriptures because you think they give you eternal life. But the Scriptures point to me!" Here, Jesus reveals the deeper purpose of the Torah and the entirety of scripture, positioning them as a divine narrative that ultimately points toward him. Far more than a collection of laws and teachings, the Torah is part of a grand design that prepares humanity for the arrival of the Messiah.

This exploration invites a deeper dive into the intricate word formation of "Torah" in the Hebrew language, uncovering the profound mysteries that God has embedded within its very structure. The term "Torah" is far more than a simple designation for the sacred text; it is a word rich with layers of meaning that reveal divine wisdom and purpose. Each aspect of its etymology and linguistic roots, points to its function as a source of instruction, guidance, and divine teaching. By examining the Hebrew letters, their arrangement, and their connections to broader scriptural truths, one begins to perceive the depth of God's intentionality in choosing this word to describe His law and teachings. This study aims to unravel the spiritual significance encoded within the Torah, shedding light on how its very name reflects its role as a channel for divine revelation and a map leading humanity toward understanding God's will and ultimate plan. Through this lens, the Torah emerges not merely as a text but as a divine masterpiece, brimming with hidden treasures waiting to be discovered.

### Letter Tav (ת)

The letter Tav (ת), the final character in the Hebrew alphabet and the 22nd in its sequence, Historically, Tav has been recognized as a mark or sign, often associated with the concept of a covenant. In its ancient pictographic form, it resembled a simple cross or an intersecting mark, symbolizing completion, sealing, or a definitive agreement.

***"A Cross"***

### Letter Vav (ו)

The letter *Vav* (ו), the sixth character in the Hebrew alphabet. In its earliest form, *Vav* was depicted as a nail or peg, a symbol rich with connotations of connection, stability, and binding. This imagery reflects the practical role of a nail or peg in securing structures, anchoring elements together, or joining separate parts into a unified whole.

***"Nail"***

### Letter Resh (ר)

The letter *Resh* (ר), the twentieth character of the Hebrew alphabet, holds significant meaning both in its symbolic representation and its role within the language. In the ancient script, *Resh* was depicted as a head, a symbol that conveys profound ideas of leadership, authority, and the beginning or origin of something significant. The association with being "first" aligns with its representation of prominence and precedence, often pointing to something of primary importance or foundational value.

### *“The Head”*

## Letter Hey (ה)

The letter *Hey* (ה), the fifth character in the sequence of the Hebrew alphabet, carries rich and evocative meaning both in its symbolism and its ancient depiction. In early scripts, *Hey* was represented by the image of a person standing with arms raised upward, an expressive posture that conveys a sense of awe, wonder, and attention. This visual representation is often interpreted as an exclamation of "Lo!" or "Behold!," a call to observe or recognize something of great significance.

### *"Lo!" or "Behold!"*

*Putting all together the word "Torah" (תּוֹרָה) provides a powerful meaning “Lo! Your Head (Jesus Christ) is Nailed to the Cross”*

When the individual letters of the word "Torah" (תּוֹרָה) are combined and their symbolic meanings are understood, they unveil a powerful and deeply spiritual message: This profound interpretation aligns directly with the words of Jesus in the Gospel of John 5:39, where He declares, "You search the Scriptures because you think they give you eternal life. But the Scriptures point to me!" The word "Torah," when viewed through this lens, is not merely a term denoting the law or instruction; it becomes a prophetic declaration embedded in the fabric of God’s divine revelation. Furthermore, the word Torah, along with all sacred writings, weaves a unified narrative that reveals Christ at its heart, demonstrating that the message of salvation and the cross is present throughout the scriptures, from the very beginning to their culmination.

## Moses: A Reflection of the Law

Moses stands as a vivid representation of the Law, serving not merely as its recipient but as a living analogy of its nature, purpose, and limitations. This connection goes beyond the momentous event of God giving the law to Moses on Mount Sinai; it extends into the very fabric of Moses' life. God's divine choice of Moses was not arbitrary; it was intentional, designed to reveal deeper truths about the law. Through Moses, God not only delivered His commandments but also wove into the narrative of his life a mysterious and profound illustration and design of the Law and what the law is capable of accomplishing and, equally, where its limitations lie.

### Moses: A reflection of the law

Moses is uniquely described in scripture as the most humble man on earth, a testimony given directly by God Himself. This remarkable statement is found in the book of Numbers 12:3 (NKJV), which declares, "Now the man Moses was very humble, more than all men who were on the face of the earth." This divine affirmation of Moses' character is not limited to his personal humility but is also reflected in his deep compassion and intercession for the people of Israel. Time and again, Moses stood as a mediator between God and the Israelites, demonstrating his profound love and sense of responsibility for the people entrusted to his care.

One of the most striking examples of this is found during the incident of the golden calf, as recounted in Exodus 32. When the Israelites sinned by creating and worshiping the golden calf, Moses, understanding the gravity of their rebellion, pleaded with God for their forgiveness. In a moment of extraordinary selflessness, Moses said to God in Exodus 32:32 (NKJV), "Yet now, if You will forgive their sin - but if not, I pray, blot me out of Your book which You have written." This was not a casual statement but a sincere expression of his willingness to sacrifice his own place in God's plan if it meant sparing the people from destruction.

At the same time, God, angered by the Israelites' stubbornness, referred to them as a stiff-necked people and declared His intention to destroy them and create a new nation from Moses. As written in Exodus 32:9-10 (NKJV), "And the Lord said to Moses, 'I have seen this people, and indeed it is a stiff-necked people! Now therefore, let Me alone, that My wrath may burn hot against them and I may consume them. And I will make of you a great nation.'" Yet Moses, embodying the heart of a true shepherd and spiritual father, interceded passionately on their behalf, pleading for God's mercy. His fervent prayer moved God to relent and spare the Israelites from destruction.

This extraordinary episode not only highlights Moses' humility but also reveals the depth of his love and commitment to the people of Israel. Like a father for his children, Moses bore their burdens, stood in the gap between their failings and God's justice, and continually sought their restoration, even at great personal cost. His life serves as a powerful example of humility, selflessness, and a heart deeply aligned with God's purposes.

In a similar way to how Moses was appointed to guide the Israelites, providing correction and direction as they journeyed toward the Promised Land, his role served as a divine instrument to lead them according to God's purpose, Law was given to guide and instruct humanity, it was designed to reveal the heart of the Father and His desires for His creation. The Law serves as a divine guide, offering direction, correction, and illumination on the path of righteousness. It provides a moral compass and helps humanity understand what it means to walk in alignment with God's will. This purpose is beautifully captured in Proverbs 6:23 (NKJV): "For the commandment is a lamp, and the law a light; Reproofs of instruction are the way of life."

The commandments act as a lamp, shining light on the path of life, ensuring that humanity is not left wandering in darkness. The reproofs of instruction, while corrective, are essential for leading people toward a fulfilling life in harmony with God's design. The Law, in this sense, was never intended as a burden but as a means of guidance, demonstrating the Father's care in pointing humanity toward a life of holiness, wisdom, and communion with Him.

*Moses served as a profound metaphor for the Law, embodying its tireless dedication and unyielding perseverance in guiding humanity toward fellowship with the Father. His life and role vividly illustrate the law as a way, striving to reconcile a broken relationship between God and His people.*

**Moses: A Levi**

Moses, born to parents from the tribe of Levi, came into the world during a time of great oppression under Pharaoh's decree to kill Hebrew male infants. As recorded in Exodus 2:1-2 (NKJV), "A man of the house of Levi went and took as wife, a daughter of Levi. So the woman conceived and bore a son." To protect him, his mother hid him for three months and then set him afloat in a basket on the Nile. Pharaoh's daughter discovered and adopted him, unknowingly hiring his own mother as his nurse.

Jacob, the patriarch of Israel, was the father of twelve sons who became the founders of the twelve tribes of Israel. Levi, the third son born to Jacob and Leah, became the ancestor of the tribe of Levi, a family uniquely designated for priestly service and sacred duties in Israel. Yet, the circumstances of Levi's birth reveal a deeper, more profound narrative. The Bible describes how Jacob loved Rachel more than Leah, as reflected in Genesis 29:30 (NKJV): "Then Jacob also went in to Rachel, and he also loved Rachel more than Leah." Jacob had been tricked by Laban into marrying Leah, Rachel's older sister, instead of Rachel, the woman he cherished. As a result, Levi was born to a wife who was not Jacob's choice, a detail that carries significant symbolic meaning.

This scenario serves as a meaningful analogy for the origin of the Law. Levi, born to Jacob through Leah - whom Jacob was deceived into marrying, as described in Genesis 29:25 (NKJV): "So it came to pass in the morning, that behold, it was Leah. And he said to Laban, 'What is this you have done to me? Was it not for Rachel that I served you? Why then have you deceived me?'" - illustrates the connection between deception and its consequences. Similarly, the Law was introduced because Adam was deceived by the serpent into eating from the Tree of the Knowledge of Good and Evil. This transgression resulted in humanity's fall into sin, necessitating the establishment of the Law to address the resulting separation from God. The Levites, as descendants of Levi, symbolize this connection, representing the Law that arose to guide humanity back toward God.

*Levi's birth to a wife who was not loved serves as a symbolic parallel to the origin of the Law, which arose from the Tree of the Knowledge of Good and Evil, a tree God did not desire humanity to partake of.*

## Moses's Father in law

Moses's father-in-law, a priest of Midian, was known for his wisdom and hospitality. After Moses fled Egypt, he was welcomed into his household and lived there for many years. During this time, Moses served his father-in-law by tending his flocks, working as a shepherd in the wilderness. His father in law has three names in the bible, Jethro, Reuel and Hobab.

## Jethro

Jethro, one of the names attributed to Moses's father-in-law as mentioned in Exodus 3:1 (NKJV) "Now Moses was tending the flock of Jethro his father-in-law," carries the profound meaning of "His Excellence," a title that conveys honor, dignity, and greatness. This name is symbolic and serves as a representation of God the Father within the triune relationship. Just as the Father in the Trinity embodies supreme authority and power, so does the name Jethro reflect an aspect of divine excellence. This parallel is supported by the declaration of God in Genesis 17:1 (NKJV), where He reveals Himself to Abraham, saying, "I am Almighty God." The name Jethro, therefore, echoes the majesty and sovereignty of God the Father, underscoring His role as the ultimate source of wisdom, strength, and authority.

***Jethro - "His Excellence" - represents Father God***

## Reuel

Reuel, another name for Moses's father-in-law, appears in the biblical account in Exodus 2:17-19 (NKJV), where he is described as the father of the women Moses helps at the well. The passage recounts how shepherds attempted to drive the women away, but Moses intervened, defending them and watering their flock. When the women returned home, Reuel, their father, asked, "How is it that you have come so soon today?" The name Reuel holds deep spiritual significance, meaning "God shall pasture." This name symbolizes the guiding and nurturing role of the Holy Spirit.

In a broader spiritual context, Reuel's name reflects the work of the Holy Spirit, who, like a shepherd, leads and pastures the hearts of believers, drawing them closer to the truth of Jesus Christ. This aligns with the teaching found in 1 Corinthians 12:3 (NKJV), which states, "No one can say that Jesus is Lord except by the Holy Spirit." The Holy Spirit acts as the divine guide, revealing the truth of Christ and empowering individuals to know Him as Lord and Savior.

***Reuel - "God shall pasture" - represents Holy Spirit***

**Hobab**

Hobab, another name associated with Moses's father-in-law, is mentioned in the biblical account found in Judges 4:11 (NKJV): "Now Heber the Kenite, of the children of Hobab the father-in-law of Moses." The name Hobab carries the significant meaning of "beloved," a term that reflects deep affection, honor, and intimacy. This name symbolically points to Jesus Christ, the Son of God, who is described as the "Beloved" by the Father. This connection is beautifully expressed during the baptism of Jesus, as recorded in Matthew 3:17 (NKJV), where a voice from heaven declares, "This is My beloved Son, in whom I am well pleased."

***Hobab - "Beloved" - represents Jesus Christ***

**In a Nutshell MOSES'S FATHER-IN-LAW**

*The names of Moses's father-in-law, Jethro, meaning "His Excellence," Reuel, meaning "God shall pasture," and Hobab, meaning "Beloved," symbolize the triune nature of God. These names suggest that Moses married a wife who came from a family symbolically tied to the triune God. Symbolizing Law (Moses) is covenanted to Adam (Moses's Wife) who came from Triune God (Moses's Father-in-Law).*

## Moses's Wife

When Moses fled from Egypt to Midian, he found refuge in the household of Jethro, a Midianite priest. Jethro not only provided Moses with a safe haven but also gave him his daughter, Zipporah, in marriage. This significant event is recorded in Exodus 2:21 (NKJV): "Then Moses was content to live with the man, and he gave Zipporah, his daughter to Moses." The name

Zipporah carries the meaning of "bird" or "beauty," a term that holds deep symbolic resonance.

The name Zipporah is seen as a metaphor with profound spiritual meaning, connecting to Adam. When God created Adam, He made him in His own image and saw him as His beloved creation, full of innocence, beauty, and potential. In God's eyes, Adam was a cherished child, perfect and adorable, with the freedom to explore and choose his path according to his heart's desires. This divine gift of free will reflected God's trust in Adam. In a similar way, the name Zipporah embodies qualities of beauty and freedom, much like a bird that soars and explores without restraint. Her role as Moses's wife metaphorically mirrors the relationship between Adam and God.

**Husband of blood**

Moses spent forty years in the land of Midian, living with his father-in-law and his wife, Zipporah. During this time, he worked as a shepherd, tending the flocks of his father-in-law. Meanwhile, the Israelites groaned under the heavy burden of slavery in Egypt, and God remembered His covenant with Abraham, Isaac, and Jacob. In response, He came down to deliver them. God revealed Himself to Moses at Mount Horeb through the burning bush, a miraculous encounter that occurred while Moses was tending sheep. During this divine meeting, God called Moses to return to Egypt, promising that through him, He would deliver the Israelites from bondage.

After receiving God's commission, Moses spoke with his father- in-law, Jethro, explaining God's plan to free His people. Jethro, in wisdom and understanding, sent Moses on his way in peace. Moses then set out for Egypt with his wife and children, obedient to the mission God had given him. However, along the journey, a startling event occurred: the Lord met Moses with the intent to kill him. In this critical moment, Zipporah took a sharp stone, circumcised her son, and cast the foreskin at Moses' feet, declaring, "You are a husband of blood!" as recorded in Exodus 4:26 (NKJV).

Zipporah's marriage to Moses, and her dramatic declaration of him as a "husband of blood," carries a profound spiritual analogy. It reflects humanity's relationship with the Law through Adam, who, by transgressing God's command and eating from the Tree of the Knowledge of Good and Evil, became bound to the Law. This binding parallels Zipporah's relationship with Moses, where the term "husband of blood" symbolizes the demands of the Law, which require bloodshed for atonement when the law (Moses) attempts to deliver the children of God from Egypt (oppression).

The phrase "husband of blood" signifies the unyielding justice of the Law, a system that, once introduced, required sacrifices to reconcile humanity's sins. This is illustrated in the book of Exodus 30:10 (NKJV), which states, "And Aaron shall make atonement upon its horns once a year with the blood of the sin offering of atonement." The Law's requirement for blood offerings underlines its role in exposing sin and demanding restitution, a reality that began with Adam's fall. In Adam, humanity entered into a marriage covenant to the Law, a covenant that necessitates the shedding of blood to satisfy divine justice.

Zipporah married to Moses and calling him the "husband of blood," is an analogy of humanity in Adam married to the Law, when Adam transgressed by eating from the tree of knowledge of good and evil. The meaning of husband of blood refers to the requirement of the bloodshed in the law as mentioned in the book of Exodus 30:10 (NKJV) "And Aaron shall make atonement upon its horns once a year with the blood of the sin offering of atonement"

## In a Nutshell

## Zipporah

*In Adam, humanity was created as precious and beautiful in the eyes of God, endowed with the freedom to live and thrive, like a bird soaring unbound. However, through transgression, humanity entered into a binding relationship with the Law, a union that was never the will of the Father. This relationship turned the Law into a "husband of blood," demanding an atonement for sin.*

### Moses's First Son

When Moses married Zipporah, she bore him a son, whom he named Gershom. This is recorded in Exodus 2:22 (NKJV): “He called his name Gershom, for he said, ‘I have been a stranger in a foreign land.’” The name Gershom, which literally means "stranger," reflects Moses's personal experience of fleeing his homeland in Egypt and living as an exile in the unfamiliar land of Midian for forty years. The name encapsulates Moses's sense of displacement, his identity as a sojourner, and his journey in a land far from the place of his birth and upbringing.

This narrative resonates deeply with the story of Adam, the first man, who also found himself as a stranger in a foreign land. When Adam transgressed against God by eating from the Tree of the Knowledge of Good and Evil, he was cast out of the Garden of Eden, a place of perfect communion with the Father and dominion over all creation. The garden, designed as Adam's home and the center of his fellowship with God, became a lost paradise. Sent out into a strange and fallen world, Adam no longer had the direct and intimate fellowship with God that he once enjoyed.

The birth of Gershom, the fruit of Moses and Zipporah's union, serves as a symbolic parallel to humanity's journey in Adam. Just as Gershom's name reflects status as a stranger, humanity in Adam became exiled from the garden, entering a foreign and unfamiliar land. This exile occurred because of Adam's covenant-like relationship with the Law, which began when he ate from the forbidden tree. This transgression bound humanity to the Law, much like a marriage covenant, and brought about separation from God.

Gershom's name becomes a poignant reminder of humanity's fallen state, their estrangement from the Father, and their journey in a land not meant to be their home. It highlights the longing for restoration and reconciliation, pointing toward the hope of returning to the fellowship and dominion that were lost in the garden. Through this analogy, Gershom represents the condition of humanity, displaced yet yearning for redemption and a restored relationship with God.

## Moses's Second Son

After Moses returned to Egypt by God's command, he led the Israelites out of bondage with the mighty hand of God. They journeyed toward freedom, eventually encamping at Sinai, the mountain of God. It was there, in the wilderness, that Moses' father-in-law, Jethro, came to meet him, bringing along Moses's wife, Zipporah, and his two sons, Gershom and Eliezer. This is recorded in Exodus 18:5 (NKJV): "Jethro, Moses' father-in-law, came with his sons and his wife to Moses in the wilderness, where he was encamped at the mountain of God."

The name of Moses's second son, Eliezer, holds another deep significance, meaning "My God is Help." This meaning is explained in Exodus 18:4 (NKJV), where Moses said, "The name of the other was Eliezer (for he said, 'The God of my father was my help, and delivered me from the sword of Pharaoh')." By naming his son Eliezer, Moses commemorated the divine intervention that saved his life when he fled Egypt, escaping Pharaoh's wrath and the threat of death.

This story parallels the role of the Law, which was given to humanity as a guide to help them navigate the darkness caused by their separation from God. The book of Hebrews 10:1 (NKJV) describes this limited role: "For the law, having a shadow of the good things to come, and not the very image of the things, can never with these same sacrifices, which they offer continually year by year, make those who approach perfect." While the Law could not restore perfect fellowship with the Father, it served as a shadow, a glimpse of goodness and light, offering humanity a path to escape the terrors of sin and darkness.

In this sense, Eliezer's name becomes an analogy for the Law's purpose. Just as Moses recognized God's help in delivering him from Pharaoh's sword, the Law was given to humanity to illuminate a way out of the darkness brought on by sin. However, just as the Law offered only a shadow and not complete restoration, the light it provided could not deliver humanity from utter darkness. The Law pointed to the need for a greater help and deliverer, one who would bring true light and permanent reconciliation with the Father God. Eliezer's name, therefore, stands as a reminder of God's help in times of deliverance while also foreshadowing humanity's deeper need for redemption beyond what the Law alone could provide.

## In a Nutshell

## MOSES FAMILY

*A closer look at Moses's family reveals profound spiritual symbolism, where each member reflects a hidden message about God's divine relationship with humanity. Moses's father-in- law represents the triune God through his names: Jethro ("His Excellence"), symbolizing the Father; Reuel ("God shall pasture"), reflecting the Spirit's guidance; and Hobab ("Beloved"), pointing to the Son, Jesus Christ.*

*Moses, descended from Levi, the son of Leah - the unloved wife - symbolizes how the Law arose not as God's ultimate will but as a response to humanity's imperfection. Zipporah, Moses's wife, whose name means "beauty" or "bird," mirrors how God saw Adam: innocent, beautiful, and free, created in His image. Gershom, Moses's first son, meaning "stranger," represents Adam's fall and estrangement from God when he was cast out of Eden into a foreign land after disobedience.*

*Eliezer, Moses's second son, whose name means "My God is Help," reflects God's enduring love for humanity. Though separated by their own will, God gave the Law as a guide, allowing mankind to see a shadow of His goodness. Together, the lives of Moses's family members serve as a divine illustration of Law and its bond to humanity.*

## Exodus - Journey with Moses

During the Exodus journey of the Israelites, from their deliverance from Egypt to the death of Moses, numerous events unfolded, each reflecting the purpose and limitations of the Law. Among these, several key moments highlighted the purpose and function of the Law given to Moses. Events such as the parting of the Red Sea, the giving of the Ten Commandments at Mount Sinai, Water from the Rock, Manna, building of Tabernacle, Moses's death at Mount Nebo, etc. These events illustrated that the Law was designed to govern, guide, and convict, but it could not redeem or transform. Instead, the Law pointed forward to the grace and salvation that would later be fulfilled through Jesus Christ. This exploration will focus on two key events that frame the Exodus journey, the beginning with the Red Sea crossing and the conclusion with the death of Moses in Deuteronomy.

### Red Sea crossing

The account of the Israelites crossing the Red Sea is detailed in Exodus chapter 14. Following the death of the firstborn in Egypt, Pharaoh, overwhelmed by the devastating plague, finally released the children of Israel along with their women, children, and livestock. This marked the beginning of Israel's deliverance from bondage. In commemoration of this momentous event, Moses proclaimed the Feast of Unleavened Bread, commanding the Israelites to observe it as a remembrance of their exodus and God's deliverance from slavery.

As the Israelites set out on their journey of freedom, they followed God's guidance and camped at Pi Hahiroth, located between Migdol and the Red Sea, directly opposite Baal Zephon, exactly as God had instructed. This strategic positioning, however, would soon serve as the stage for one of the most miraculous acts of deliverance recorded in Scripture.

Meanwhile, Pharaoh and his officials, gripped by regret and stubbornness, hardened their hearts once more. Unable to accept the loss of their labor force, they assembled their army, including chariots and horsemen, and set out in pursuit of the Israelites. When the Israelites saw the advancing Egyptian army, fear gripped their hearts, and they cried out to Moses in panic and despair, accusing him of leading them into the wilderness to die. In their desperation, they questioned God's plan and Moses' leadership, momentarily forgetting the miracles God had already performed on their behalf.

Despite their fear, Moses remained steadfast and called upon the Lord. God responded by instructing Moses to lift his rod and stretch his hand over the sea. As Moses obeyed, the waters of the Red Sea miraculously parted, forming walls of water on both sides, creating a dry path for the Israelites to cross. With faith and courage, the Israelites passed through the sea on dry ground, escaping the Egyptian forces that pursued them.

However, when Pharaoh's army attempted to follow them into the sea, God intervened once again, as the Israelites safely reached the other side, Moses stretched his rod once more, and the waters of the sea returned to their place, engulfing Pharaoh's army and destroying them completely. Not a single Egyptian survived.

**Jordan Crossing**

The account of the Israelites crossing the Jordan River is detailed in Joshua chapter 3. After wandering in the wilderness for forty years, the children of Israel finally stood at the threshold of the Promised Land, prepared to cross the Jordan River and step into the inheritance God had promised to Abraham, Isaac, and Jacob. With Moses having passed away, Joshua was now the appointed leader, tasked with guiding the nation into Canaan.

As the Israelites approached the Jordan River, God reassured Joshua that He would perform yet another miracle to demonstrate His power and faithfulness, just as He had parted the Red Sea for their forefathers. Joshua instructed the priests to carry the Ark of the Covenant, which represented God's presence, and lead the people to the river's edge. The people were commanded to sanctify themselves, as God was about to do wonders in their midst. As the priests' feet touched the water, the flow of the Jordan stopped, and the waters stood still, piling up at a distance, leaving dry ground for the Israelites to cross.

The entire nation of Israel passed through the Jordan River on dry land, just as their ancestors had crossed the Red Sea. In obedience to God's command, twelve men, one from each tribe of Israel, carried stones from the riverbed and set them up as a memorial at Gilgal. Once everyone had crossed safely, the priests carrying the Ark of the Covenant came up from the river, and the waters of the Jordan returned to their place, flowing as they had before.

### What's the difference

The crossing of the Red Sea marked a pivotal moment in the Exodus journey of the Israelites, as they walked away from their bondage in Egypt and witnessed the destruction of their oppressors. In Hebrew, the word for Egypt is "Matsor" (the dual form of "Mitsrayim"), which, according to Hebrew Strong's Concordance #4693, means "distress," "confinement," or "siege." This word is derived from the Hebrew root verb צור (tsur), implying a state of being trapped or pressed in. The exodus from Egypt, led by Moses, serves as a profound analogy of how the Law functions to lead humanity - which, in Adam, was confined under the siege of sin - away from its fallen state and into freedom.

Moses, representing the Law, guided the Israelites through the Red Sea, symbolizing an effort to separate humanity from the bondage of sin. Yet, despite this deliverance, the Law was unable to complete the journey to the Promised Land, leaving the people to wander in the wilderness. This foreshadows the limitations of the Law, which can reveal sin but cannot provide redemption or salvation. Instead, the Law prepares the way for the grace that comes through Jesus Christ.

The fulfillment of entering the Promised Land came under the leadership of Joshua, whose name in Hebrew - Yehoshua (יְהוֹשֻׁעַ) - means "The Lord is Salvation" or "Yahweh Saves." This name was later shortened to Yeshua (יֵשׁוּעַ) and translated into Greek as Iēsous (Ἰησοῦς), eventually becoming Jesus in English. When Joshua and the priests carrying the Ark of the Covenant stepped into the Jordan River, the waters parted, making a way for Israel to enter their inheritance. Joshua's leadership in leading Israel across the Jordan River into Canaan, mirrors Jesus Christ's role in leading humanity into the eternal Promised Land - the Kingdom of God and eternal life.

This parallel is emphasized in Romans 8:3 (NKJV): "For what the law could not do in that it was weak through the flesh, God did by sending His own Son in the likeness of sinful flesh, on account of sin: He condemned sin in the flesh." The Law, though holy and righteous, was unable to save humanity because it depended on the weakness of the flesh. It pointed out sin but could not redeem. Jesus Christ, however, came in the likeness of sinful flesh, taking the penalty of sin upon Himself and providing the grace and salvation that the Law could only foreshadow.

Thus, the leadership of Moses and Joshua illustrates the contrast between the Law and Grace. The Law reveals the need for salvation, while Jesus, the greater Joshua, fulfills that need by leading humanity into the eternal inheritance promised by God.

## Moses's Death

After Moses led the children of Israel to the plains of Moab, he ascended from there to Mount Nebo, reaching the summit of Pisgah, which lies directly across from Jericho. From this elevated vantage point, the Lord revealed to Moses the vast expanse of the Promised Land - the land He had solemnly promised to give to Abraham, Isaac, and Jacob as an inheritance for their descendants.

## Moses's Countenance

Moses was one hundred and twenty years old at the time of his death on Mount Nebo. Despite his advanced age, scripture emphasizes that his eyesight remained clear and his physical strength was undiminished. This remarkable detail is recorded in Deuteronomy 34:7 (NKJV): "Moses was one hundred and twenty years old when he died. His eyes were not dim nor his natural vigor diminished." This description highlights that Moses' physical condition did not deteriorate with age, symbolizing a lasting strength and enduring vitality even at the end of his life.

This account serves as a spiritual parallel to the Law of God, which Moses represents. Just as Moses' vision remained clear and his vigor unbroken, the Law is holy, perfect, and unchanging. It reflects the standard of God's righteousness, as described in Romans 7:12 (NKJV): "Therefore the law is holy, and the commandment holy and just and good." The Law, much like Moses, retains its purity and perfection without decay or diminishment over time.

However, while the Law reveals God's standard of holiness, it does not have the power to make humanity holy or save them from sin. It serves to expose sin and point to the need for grace and redemption through Jesus Christ. Moses, as a representation of the Law, could lead the Israelites to the border of the Promised Land but could not take them in, illustrating the Law's limitation in bringing salvation.

## Moses's burial

Moses holds a unique distinction in the history of humanity, as he is the only person whom God Himself buried. This extraordinary act is recorded in Deuteronomy 34:6 (NKJV): "And He buried him in a valley in the land of Moab, opposite Beth Peor; but no one knows his grave to this day." Unlike any other individual, Moses' burial was carried out directly by God, and the location of his grave remains unknown, emphasizing the divine purpose and mystery surrounding his death and burial.

This divinely orchestrated burial of Moses serves as a symbolic representation of the Law, which Moses personifies. The Law, given through Moses, represents the covenant that Adam unknowingly established with God by reaching out and eating 141 from the Tree of the Knowledge of Good and Evil in the garden of Eden.

Through this act, Adam entered into a state of accountability to the standard of righteousness, bringing humanity under the expectations of the Law.

Just as God buried Moses, ensuring that no human hand could alter or dishonor his final resting place, the Law, too, was fulfilled and set aside through the death and resurrection of Jesus Christ. Humanity could not bury or abolish the Law by its own efforts; it was God's sovereign act to fulfill and seal its purpose in Christ. Jesus accomplished the purpose of the Law, satisfying its righteous requirements. In this way, the burial of Moses parallels the end of the Law's reign over humanity, making room for the new covenant established through Jesus Christ.

Thus, the burial of Moses by God Himself highlights the completion of the Law's purpose and directs all of humanity to look toward Jesus Christ, who fulfilled the Law and brought redemption through His sacrifice.

## Buried in Moab

The birth of Moab is recorded in the book of Genesis 19:30-38. After the destruction of Sodom and Gomorrah, Lot and his two daughters fled to the mountains and took refuge in a cave out of fear. Believing that there were no men left on earth to continue their family line, Lot's daughters devised a plan to preserve their father's lineage. They made their father drink wine, and each lay with him without his knowledge. As a result, both daughters conceived and gave birth to sons. The older daughter bore a son named Moab, whose descendants became the Moabites, a people group that later inhabited the region east of the Jordan River.

The birth of Moab carries a profound symbolic parallel to the birth of the Law into humanity. Just as Lot's daughters betrayed their father, leading to the birth of Moab, the transgression of Adam and Eve against the heavenly Father brought forth the Law into the human experience. They acted in defiance of God's command stepping into a covenantal relationship which is the Law. Here, the birth of Moab and the introduction of law into humanity are metaphorical.

Looking into the life of Moses, he is the figurative representation of the law, which could not save mankind. Now Moses, who symbolizes the Law, is buried by God in Moab, the land that figuratively represents the origin of the Law. Thereby, God put an end to the Law that separated God and mankind. This analogy illustrates that God brought the Law to its conclusion at the very place that symbolized its origin.

This parallel between the birth of Moab and the Law highlights how both emerged from a foundation of deception, human ignorance and failure, yet were ultimately buried by God to make way for redemption and new beginnings. Just as Moses' burial in Moab marked the end of the Law's authority, Jesus Christ fulfilled the Law and provided life, leading humanity into the spiritual Promised Land.

## Summary

The Law, which was given by God, was not the original plan in His heart for humanity but was instituted as a result of man's choice through Adam in the Garden of Eden. While the Law is holy, righteous, and good, it was never designed to make humanity holy or to grant salvation. Instead, its purpose was to highlight humanity's shortcomings, and measure their righteousness against the perfect standard of God.

However, in this evaluation, mankind was always found lacking, unable to meet the requirements of the Law through their own efforts. The Law, by its very nature, reflects the holiness of God and demands perfection, a standard that fallen humanity cannot attain without Jesus. As stated in Romans 3:20 (NKJV): "Therefore by the deeds of the law no flesh will be justified in His sight, for by the law is the knowledge of sin."

The life of Moses serves as a symbolic representation of the Law, highlighting its purpose, limitations, and role in pointing humanity toward the promises of God. Moses, like the Law, was divinely given to lead and instruct, revealing our status with the Father God and setting the standard of righteousness. However, just as Moses could lead the Israelites to the border of the Promised Land but could not take them in, the Law exposes humanity's inability to achieve salvation through their own righteousness.

The burial of Moses by God Himself in the land of Moab symbolizes the end of the Law's authority, as it pointed to the need for a Savior - Jesus Christ - who fulfilled the Law and became the way and salvation for the entire humanity. This illustrates that the Law was not meant to save humanity but to show you who you are and your need for Christ, the true deliverer, who leads humanity into the eternal inheritance promised by God.

**Take Away**

The life of Moses offers a compelling demonstration of how God intricately embedded His overarching plan within the framework of the Law. Each scripture within the Law is rich with hidden treasures and deeper truths that ultimately point to Jesus Christ as their fulfillment. To fully grasp the essence of these scriptures, it is essential to approach them with both curiosity and humility, seeking God's wisdom to view them through His divine perspective rather than through the lens of human limitation.

For many, the portrayal of God in the Old Testament often seems at odds with the character of Jesus revealed in the New Testament. For instance, in Deuteronomy 5:9 (NKJV), God declares, "I, the Lord your God, am a jealous God, visiting the iniquity of the fathers upon the children to the third and fourth generations of those who hate Me." This depiction of a jealous and just God may appear starkly contrasting to Jesus' teaching in Matthew 5:44 (NKJV), where He says, "Love your enemies, bless those who curse you, do good to those who hate you, and pray for those who spitefully use you and persecute you." Such apparent contrasts can lead to misunderstandings about God's unchanging nature. However, by looking at scripture through God's eyes -

seeking to understand His heart and intent - these seeming contradictions but God is never changing and Jesus is the exact representation of the Father God.

Understanding the Law through God's perspective requires a shift from a literal or legalistic reading to a relational and redemptive approach. It invites the reader to ask, "What is God revealing about Himself and His eternal plan through this command?" The Law is not merely a set of rules but a divine invitation to uncover the treasures of God's wisdom and character. As Proverbs 25:2 (NKJV) reminds us, "It is the glory of God to conceal a matter, but the glory of kings is to search out a matter." This profound statement calls believers to actively seek out the truths God has intentionally woven into His Word.

Applying this understanding in daily life transforms the way one reads and engages with scripture. Instead of being overwhelmed by the complexity of the Law or misinterpreting its purpose, readers are encouraged to see each commandment as a window into God's nature and His redemptive plan. This approach nurtures a deeper relationship with God, rooted in His love, grace, and desire for reconciliation with humanity.

By exploring the Law through the lens of God's intent, believers gain a clearer understanding of His unchanging character - a God who is both holy and loving but seeking to have that intimate relationship with humanity. The Law becomes a pathway to encounter the heart of God, revealing His profound desire for humanity to live in communion with Him. Through this perspective, the scriptures come alive, leading the seeker to discover the ultimate treasure - Jesus Christ, the fulfillment of the Law and the embodiment of God's love and grace.

## My Reflection

*My son, Josiah Satish, is truly a promised child. Even before he was conceived, God gave me a promise through 1 Kings 13:2 (NKJV): "O altar, altar! Thus says the Lord: 'Behold, a child, Josiah by name, shall be born to the house of David.'" The joy we felt when he was born was immeasurable, knowing that he was a gift from God.*

*However, as he began to grow, things took an unexpected turn. He started to show signs of stubbornness, began taking things without asking, and developed a habit of lying. Watching this behavior unfold was deeply painful for both my wife and me. I found myself dwelling on these struggles, worrying about what k ind of adult he might become.*

*In the midst of my frustration, I spent time reflecting on the love of the Father, and my wife gently reminded me of something I had overlooked - I had been too strict, imposing rules and expectations on him, believing that rigid discipline would mold his character. That moment of self-realization led me to shift my perspective. Instead of looking at my son through the lens of fear, I began to see him through the promise God had given me.*

*I made a conscious decision to trust God's promise and to parent him with love and grace rather than the burden of rules and regulations. As I began to give him freedom and encourage him in faith, I witnessed an amazing transformation. His character and attitude began to change remarkably, and most importantly, his relationship with God deepened.*

*One example that touched me deeply was something he wrote in his meditation plan about John the Baptist: "No matter how highly you are in the world, you will still have to be someone who prays and worships God. Just like when John the Baptist was highly thought of by his followers, but was not sure about baptizing Jesus, because John knew that he should be the one to be baptized by Him, but because Jesus wanted him to do it and it was what God wanted."*

*This moment made me realize seeing through God's promise and the beauty of raising children through love and grace rather than the weight of the Law. By trusting God's plan and guiding them with faith, we can see amazing growth and spiritual maturity in our children. Josiah's journey has been a living testimony of what happens when we let go of fear, lean into God's promises, and allow grace to lead the way.*

# Chapter - 5
# TEN PLAGUES OF EGYPT

## Introduction

When Moses returned to Egypt from the land of Midian, he was eighty years old, answering God's call to lead the Israelites out of their bondage. The Book of Exodus details the ten plagues that God brought upon the Egyptians to compel Pharaoh to release His people. These plagues, which included turning the Nile's waters into blood, swarms of frogs, flies, locusts, devastating hail, and ultimately the death of Egypt's firstborn. This significant event is referenced in various parts of the Bible. For instance, Psalm 78:43-51 poetically recounts the plagues.

The question arises: Did God bring these plagues solely to display His power? In Exodus 9:16 (NKJV), God speaks directly to Pharaoh, saying, "But indeed for this purpose I have raised you up, that I may show My power in you, and that My name may be declared in all the earth." This statement states that God's intent was to demonstrate His supreme authority and ensure that His name would be known among the nations. Yet, the Bible also reveals God's compassionate nature. In Ezekiel 33:11 (NKJV), God states, "As I live,' says the Lord God, 'I have no pleasure in the death of the wicked, but that the wicked turn from his way and live." This highlights that God does not take joy in destruction but desires repentance and restoration.

The ten plagues carry a deeper metaphorical meaning, representing the loss humanity suffered through Adam's transgression and separation from God. When Adam transgressed by eating from the Tree of the Knowledge of Good and Evil, humanity fell into a state of brokenness, losing communion with the Father. The plagues reflect the journey of humanity's loss: the turning of water into blood symbolizes the loss of life and purity, while the swarms of creatures, darkness, and death mirror the chaos, corruption, and separation brought about by sin. At the same time, the plagues demonstrate God's power to reverse and restore what was lost through Jesus Christ.

### Question to ponder

- Is it necessary for humanity to endure all the pain and suffering they experience today?

## First Plague: Waters Become Blood

The Lord spoke to Moses, instructing him to confront Pharaoh, whose heart remained hardened and unwilling to release the Israelites. God told Moses to meet Pharaoh in the morning by the riverbank, carrying the rod of Aaron. Moses was to deliver God's message: Exodus 7:6 (NKJV) "The Lord, the God of the Hebrews, has sent me to tell you, 'Let My people go so they may serve Me in the wilderness.' But until now, you, Pharaoh have refused to listen." Then the Lord commanded Moses to strike the water of river Nile Exodus 7:14 (NKJV) "Thus says the Lord: "By this you shall know that I am the Lord. Behold, I will strike the waters which are in the river with the rod that is in my hand, and they shall be turned to blood."

### First plague in Adam

Throughout the scriptures, water, blood, and spirit are interconnected and agree as one, as revealed in 1 John 5:8 (NKJV): "And there are three that bear witness on earth: the Spirit, the water, and the blood; and these three agree as one." This profound connection traces back to the creation of humanity. When God formed Adam from the dust of the ground, He breathed the breath of life into his nostrils, and Adam became a living being. This act signifies that Adam's life was rooted in the Spirit, aligning him with God, who created him in His own image. The nature of God is spirit, as Jesus states in John 4:24 (NKJV): "God is Spirit, and those who worship Him must worship in spirit and truth." Thus, Adam's life reflected the divine nature, living in harmony with God through the Spirit.

However, this spiritual life was disrupted when Adam transgressed against God's command in the Garden of Eden by eating from the Tree of the Knowledge of Good and Evil. Through his disobedience, Adam no longer lived by the Spirit but by the blood. His life became sustained by blood rather than the Spirit, a truth revealed in Leviticus 17:11 (NKJV): "For the life of the flesh is in the blood." This transition symbolized a profound fall from divine communion and spiritual life.

This spiritual reality is mirrored in the first plague God brought upon Egypt, where the waters of the Nile were turned into blood. Water, often symbolic of life, purity, and the Spirit, was transformed into blood, a representation of death and corruption as in the first plague resulted in death of all the fishes and living creatures in the Nile river. Just as Adam's fall caused him to forfeit the life of the Spirit for a life sustained by blood, this plague symbolized the loss of spiritual vitality and the entry of death into humanity's existence. The turning of water to blood in Egypt serves as a metaphor for the first "plague" that befell Adam: his separation in the Spirit, which brought forth death and mortality.

**First plague reversed**

The wedding at Cana in Galilee is where Jesus performed His first recorded miracle, as described in John 2:1-11. Jesus, His mother Mary, and His disciples were among the guests at a wedding celebration. During the feast, the wine supply ran out, which could have caused great embarrassment to the hosts. Mary Jesus's mother, noticing the situation, approached Jesus and said, "They have no wine." Although Jesus replied that His time had not yet come, Mary instructed the servants to follow His directions, saying, "Whatever He says to you, do it."

Jesus then told the servants to fill six large stone jars with water. Once they had done so, He instructed them to draw some out and present it to the master of the feast. To everyone's amazement, the water had been transformed into fine wine. The master of the feast, impressed by its quality, remarked to the bridegroom, "Everyone serves the good wine first, and when people have drunk freely, then the inferior wine. But you have kept the good wine until now!"

The first recorded miracle of Jesus, turning water into wine at the wedding in Cana, holds deep spiritual significance and serves as a profound symbol of humanity's restoration through the redeeming work of Christ through His blood. The wine in this miracle serves as a powerful metaphor for the blood of Jesus, which was shed to cleanse and restore humanity. This is further highlighted in Jacob's prophetic blessing over Judah, as recorded in Genesis 49:11 (NKJV): "He washed his garments in wine, and his clothes in the blood of grapes." This prophecy foreshadows the sacrificial blood of Christ, which would bring redemption and restoration, ultimately restoring humanity's spiritual life and relationship with God.

Additionally, the mention of the six large stone jars in the miracle carries significant symbolism. The number six is associated with humanity, as Adam, the first man, was created on the sixth day. The act of filling the jars with water represents humanity's emptiness and reliance on its own spirit and desires, which are inadequate to bring about true fulfillment or restoration. This inadequacy may also reflect the embarrassment of the wedding hosts running out of wine, a metaphor for humanity's lack of spiritual sufficiency.

When Jesus transforms the water into wine, it signifies being filled with the Spirit of God, represented by the wine, which also points to the blood of Jesus Christ. This transformation brings about celebration and joy, symbolizing the newness of life found in Jesus Christ. Just as the wedding feast was renewed with the best wine, humanity is offered a renewed relationship with God, filled with grace, joy, and eternal life, through the sacrifice of Jesus.

*This miracle can be understood as a metaphor for reversing the "first plague" that befell humanity. Just as the waters of the Nile were turned to blood in Egypt resulting in death, Jesus' miracle at Cana turns water into wine symbolizes reversal of the first plague, the spiritual death through his blood, a sign of life, joy, and redemption. In summary, reversing the spiritual death of humanity through his blood*

## Second Plague - Frogs

Despite the first plague, Pharaoh continued to defy God and refused to release the Israelites. In response, God spoke to Moses, warning him of the next judgment. In Exodus 8:2-4 (NKJV), God said: "But if you refuse to let them go, behold, I will strike all your territory with frogs. The river shall bring forth frogs in abundance, and they will come up into your house, your bedroom, and your bed, into the houses of your servants, on your people, into your ovens, and into your kneading bowls. The frogs shall come upon you, your people, and all your servants."

### Second plague in Adam

When God created Adam, He placed the man in the Garden of Eden with the purpose of tending and caring for the creation. God then gave him a clear command, granting permission to eat freely from every tree in the garden except for one. The Lord specifically instructed the man not to eat from the tree of the knowledge of good and evil, warning him that on the day he ate from it, he would surely die.

While Adam did not experience physical death immediately on the same day he ate from the Tree of the Knowledge of Good and Evil, a different kind of death occurred. This death was spiritual, as Adam became unclean in his spirit that separated him from the presence of God. His disobedience brought about a condition of spiritual impurity, rendering him unfit for the perfect communion he once enjoyed with his Creator.

This concept of spiritual uncleanness can be further understood through the symbolic representation of frogs in scripture. Frogs are often associated with impurity and unclean spirits, a connection seen in Revelation 16:13 (NKJV): “And I saw three unclean spirits like frogs coming out of the mouth of the dragon, out of the mouth of the beast, and out of the mouth of the false prophet.” Here, frogs are used as a metaphor for uncleanness in spirit that emerges to spread darkness and rebellion against God.

The scripture in Exodus 8:2-4 speaks of invasion by the frogs, symbolizing spiritual uncleanness in every area of human life. Frogs in the house represent defilement of the spirit of humanity, as referenced in 2 Corinthians 5:1 (NKJV) “For we know that if our earthly house, this tent, is destroyed, we have a building from God, a house not made with hands, eternal in the heavens.” Frogs in the bedroom signify uncleanliness in marital relationships, while frogs on the bed symbolize the fruit of the body, as described in Hebrews 13:4 (NKJV) “Marriage is honorable among all, and the bed undefiled.” The presence of frogs in the servants' houses points to defilement in work, and frogs on the people indicate impurity within the family. Frogs in the oven represent unclean thoughts or the mind, and those in the kneading bowl symbolize the process of shaping and forming, as seen in Hosea 7:4 (NKJV) “They are all adulterers.

Like an oven heated by a baker - He ceases stirring the fire after kneading the dough, Until it is leavened." Together, these elements reflect spiritual defilement affecting every area of human life.

The parallel is clear: just as frogs represent spiritual impurity in the book of Revelation, Adam's spirit became unclean through his transgression in the Garden of Eden. Though he remained physically alive for centuries, his spiritual death on that day signified the loss of holiness, purity, and his relationship with God.

**Second plague reversed**

Before the betrayal of Jesus Christ by Judas Iscariot, He made several promises to His disciples, one of which was the gift of the Holy Spirit. This promise is recorded in the Gospel of John 14:16-17 (NKJV): "And I will pray the Father, and He will give you another Helper, that He may abide with you forever - the Spirit of truth, whom the world cannot receive, because it neither sees Him nor knows Him; but you know Him, for He dwells with you and will be in you." Here, Jesus assured humanity of the coming of the Holy Spirit, the Spirit of Truth, who would live within them, guiding, comforting, and empowering them for all eternity. The Spirit, referred to as the Helper, would be a constant presence in their lives, enabling them to live in connection with God.

The frogs, a biblical symbol of impurity and unclean spirit across all areas of life, are metaphorically restored and purified through the work of the Holy Spirit. This transformative power is described in Titus 3:5 (NLT):

"He saved us, not because of the righteous things we had done, but because of His mercy. He washed away our sins, giving us a new birth and new life through the Holy Spirit." Through God's love, the Holy Spirit renews and regenerates, washing away sin and offering humanity a new beginning.

This renewal signifies the clean and free life that is made possible through the Holy Spirit. By His power, humanity, which was once unclean and separated from God, is restored to a state of spiritual purity. The Holy Spirit enables individuals to live the life God intended, one of righteousness and in fellowship with Him. This promise of renewal through the Spirit underscores the profound hope and transformation available to all in Christ.

The scripture in Galatians 5:16 (NKJV) states, "Walk in the Spirit, and you shall not fulfill the lust of the flesh." This verse emphasizes the importance of living in the Spirit of God to overcome the desires of the flesh. However, humanity often interprets "walking in the spirit" as something they must strive to achieve on their own, as if walking in the Spirit is solely dependent on their efforts.

Yet, another powerful scripture found in Ezekiel 36:27 (NKJV) provides deeper insight into how this walk is made possible: "I will put My Spirit within you and cause you to walk in My statutes, and you will keep My judgments and do them." This verse reveals that walking in the Spirit is not about human striving but about divine empowerment. God Himself places His Spirit within believers, enabling them to walk according to His statutes and obey His commands.

The Spirit of God works in partnership with the individual, guiding and empowering them to live in accordance with His will. It is not a task of human effort but a collaboration where the Spirit takes the lead, causing the believer to walk in Him. This partnership transforms the journey of walking in the Spirit from a burden to a process of grace and reliance on God's power. The believer is not left to struggle but is equipped by the Spirit to fulfill God's purpose, making obedience a natural outcome of a Spirit-filled life.

*Spirit of God causes you to walk in fullness of life in the way God intended you to live, reversing the state of spiritual uncleanness to walk in holiness unto God*

## Third Plague - Lice

When Pharaoh, overwhelmed by the plague of frogs, pleaded with Moses to intercede and remove them, Moses turned to the Lord in prayer. He cried out for deliverance, and the Lord honored Moses' request, bringing relief to the land by removing the frogs. However, when Pharaoh saw the respite, his heart grew hard once again, as the Lord had foretold. He refused to heed Moses and Aaron, continuing in his stubborn defiance against God's command to release the Israelites.

In response to Pharaoh's hardened heart, the Lord instructed Moses to initiate the next plague. As recorded in Exodus 8:16 (NKJV): "Say to Aaron, 'Stretch out your rod, and strike the dust of the land, so that it may become lice throughout all the land of Egypt.'" Moses conveyed the Lord's command to Aaron, who obeyed by stretching out his rod and striking the dust of the earth. Instantly, the dust transformed into lice, spreading throughout the land and afflicting both man and beast.

**Third plague in Adam**

When the serpent deceived Eve, causing her and Adam to eat from the Tree of the Knowledge of Good and Evil, a profound transformation took place within them. Their eyes were immediately opened, and they lost the divine covering that had once enveloped them. This covering, referred to as the crown of glory granted to humanity by God, is described in Psalm 8:5 (NKJV): "For You have made him a little lower than the angels, and You have crowned him with glory and honor." Stripped of this glory, they became aware of their nakedness, and their bodies were left exposed and vulnerable.

This glory, which is the divine protection and perfect harmony with God, was removed because of their transgression. Stripped of this covering, Adam and Eve were subjected to their mortality, exposing their bodies to decay, sickness, and ultimately death. The state of nakedness was not merely physical but represented a deeper spiritual vulnerability, the loss of their image of God for them.

The presence of lice on the body symbolizes this vulnerability of the human condition. Lice, parasitic and relentless, thrive on the imperfections and weaknesses of the human body. Their infestation serves as a tangible reminder of the fallen state of humanity, a direct consequence of the removal of the crown of glory. Without the divine covering, humanity became susceptible to the suffering and frailty that accompany sin. The loss of glory left Adam and his descendants exposed, emphasizing the profound impact of separation from God and the need for restoration through His grace.

**Third plague reversed**

The work of Jesus Christ brought humanity the gift of the Holy Spirit, the Helper, who purifies and renews the spirit from all impurity. This transformative power does not merely cleanse but also elevates humanity, leading them on a journey from their present state of glory to eternal glory. This profound transformation is described in 2 Corinthians 3:18 (NKJV): “But we all, with unveiled face, beholding as in a mirror the glory of the Lord, are being transformed into the same image from glory to glory, just as by the Spirit of the Lord.”

Through the partnership with the Holy Spirit, humanity is guided into walking in the Spirit, allowing this divine process to unfold. The Spirit works within, aligning humanity with the image of Christ and leading them to eternal glory. This eternal glory represents the restoration of the crown of glory, a divine covering that protects the body from corruption and decay.

This transformation is not a result of human effort but a partnership with the Spirit, who empowers and renews. By beholding the glory of the Lord, believers are being transformed into His image, restoring what was lost in the fall and preparing them for the eternal, incorruptible glory promised by God. This crown of glory signifies not just a spiritual renewal but also the ultimate redemption of the body, shielding it from mortality and decay. Through the Spirit, Jesus fulfills His redemptive work, restoring humanity to its intended state of eternal honor and perfection.

*The Spirit of God partners with us to transform us back into the eternal glory*

## Fourth Plague - Flies

God instructed Moses to deliver a clear message to Pharaoh: to release the Israelites so they could worship the Lord their God. However, Pharaoh, hardened by his own stubbornness and pride, refused to obey God's command. In response to Pharaoh's defiance, God brought another plague upon Egypt, sending swarms of flies to devastate the land. This event is described in Exodus 8:24 (NKJV): "And the Lord did so. Thick swarms of flies came into the house of Pharaoh, into his servants' houses, and into all the land of Egypt. The land was corrupted because of the swarms of flies."

These flies invaded every corner of Egypt, filling Pharaoh's palace, the homes of his servants, and the entire land, causing widespread corruption and distress. Despite the widespread devastation in Egypt, The Israelites, who lived in Goshen, were protected from this affliction. No flies were found in their territory, highlighting the distinction God made between His people and the Egyptians.

**Fourth plague in Adam**

God created Adam in His own image, granting him the authority, a reflection of God's sovereign rule. This divine authority was a key part of Adam's identity and his relationship with the Creator, enabling him as a Son of God, like a prince having authority in alignment with God's will. However, through his transgression in the Garden of Eden, Adam forfeited this authority. By yielding to the serpent's deception, he surrendered his authority and fell under the influence of Satan, the adversary.

This transfer of authority is referenced in Luke 4:6 (NKJV): "And the devil said to Him, 'All this authority I will give You, and their glory; for this has been delivered to me, and I give it to whomever I wish.'" In this passage, Satan acknowledges that the authority he possesses was not inherently his but was delivered to him, an implication of the authority originally entrusted to humanity through Adam's creation.

The flies mentioned in the plagues of Egypt are also symbolically associated with demons in Scripture. This connection is highlighted in the Gospel of Matthew 12:24 (NKJV): "Now when the Pharisees heard it they said, 'This fellow does not cast out demons except by Beelzebub, the ruler of the demons.'" In this passage, the Pharisees accused Jesus of performing miracles and casting out demons by the power of Beelzebub, a name that translates to "Lord of the Flies." Beelzebub is often interpreted as a reference to Satan or a chief demon, signifying authority over demonic forces.

Through Adam's fall, the humanity was subjected to the dominion under Satan as mentioned when Jesus said to the Pharisees in the scriptures John 8:44 (NKJV) "You are of your father the devil." It is not just about the Pharisees but to all who do not believe in Jesus Christ since they are under Satan's dominion.

**Fourth plague reversed**

During His ministry proclaiming the kingdom of God, Jesus entrusted His disciples with divine authority, empowering them to act in His name. This is vividly described in Luke 10:18-19 (NKJV): "And He said to them, 'I saw Satan fall like lightning from heaven. Behold, I give you the authority to trample on serpents and scorpions, and over all the power of the enemy, and nothing shall by any means hurt you.'" In this declaration, Jesus not only affirms His victory over the forces of darkness but also shares His authority with His disciples, equipping them to overcome the enemy's power.

However, this authority was not limited to the twelve disciples or the seventy whom He sent out; it extends to all who are His children. This gift of authority represents a restoration of the authority humanity lost through Adam's disobedience. It is a divine empowerment to fulfill the purpose and mission of God's kingdom, signifying both victory and sonship.

This act of granting authority parallels the story of the prodigal son (Luke 15:11-32). When the son returns to his father in repentance, the father not only forgives him but restores his position as a son, placing a ring on his finger. The ring is a symbol of authority and belonging, signifying the restoration of his identity within the family. In the same way, Jesus restores to His followers the authority of sonship, enabling them to walk in the power of the kingdom and in their rightful identity as children of God.

*Through this divine empowerment, Jesus reaffirms the relationship between God and His people, restoring what was lost and inviting them to share in His sonship. This authority is a testament to God's love, grace, allowing His children to walk confidently in their calling, equipped to confront and overcome the forces of darkness.*

## Fifth plague - Livestock Diseased

Pharaoh, in his continued defiance, once again hardened his heart and refused to let the children of Israel go to worship the Lord God. Despite witnessing the previous plagues and their devastating effects, his pride and stubbornness led him to resist God's command. In response to Pharaoh's unyielding attitude, the Lord instructed Moses to deliver another solemn warning. As recorded in Exodus 9:1-3 (NKJV): "Thus says the Lord God of the Hebrews: 'Let My people go, that they may serve Me. For if you refuse to let them go, and still hold them, behold, the hand of the Lord will be on your cattle in the field, on the horses, on the donkeys, on the camels, on the oxen, and on the sheep, a very severe pestilence.'"

## Fifth plague in Adam

God created Adam as more than just a being, He created him as a son and entrusted him with divine authority. Along with this authority, God gave Adam dominion over all the earth and everything He had created. This dominion is beautifully described in Psalm 8:6 (NKJV): "You have made him to have dominion over the works of Your hands; You have put all things under his feet." Adam was designed to reflect God's image, ruling as a steward over creation, carrying both responsibility and honor.

Adam's authority and dominion are clearly demonstrated in the Garden of Eden. God brought every living creature He had created to Adam, giving him the privilege of naming them. Whatever Adam called each creature became its name, as though creation awaited his decree. This act was not simply an exercise in creativity but a profound expression of the dominion and stewardship entrusted to him. Adam's ability to name each creature was a manifestation of the dominion God had given him over all creation.

Because of Adam's fall, the authority and dominion that God had originally entrusted to him were lost. As a result, all of God's creation was also subjected to futility and placed under a state of corruption. This condition is described in Romans 8:20 (NKJV): "For the creation was subjected to futility, not willingly, but because of Him who subjected it in hope." Creation itself did not choose this state of futility, but it was subjected to it as a consequence of humanity's disobedience and separation from God.

The fall of Adam brought disorder not only to humanity but also to the natural world, including the cattle of the beasts of the field, birds of the air, and creatures of the seas. These creatures, which were once under Adam's dominion and care, became affected by the consequences of sin. They now endure hardship, suffering, and decay as part of the fallen world.

**Fifth plague reversed**

Jesus Christ, who is also fully human and the Son of God, demonstrated His divine power over death by dying and rising on the third day. Through His resurrection, He put on incorruption, fulfilling the prophecy written in Psalm 16:10 (NKJV): "For You will not leave my soul in Sheol, Nor will You allow Your Holy One to see corruption." By conquering death, Jesus defied mortality and embraced immortality, becoming the first to rise from the dead in a glorified and incorruptible body.

Furthermore, the scriptures affirm that Jesus is "the firstborn from the dead, that in all things He may have the preeminence" as declared in Colossians 1:18 (NKJV). This title emphasizes that Jesus is not only the pioneer of resurrection but also the forerunner of humanity. His resurrection serves as a guarantee and sets a stage for humanity to likewise overcome death, putting on incorruption and immortality and revealed as sons of God.

The transformation of humanity into the sons of God has a profound impact, not just for mankind but for all of creation. Romans 8:19, 21 (NKJV) states: "For the earnest expectation of the creation eagerly waits for the revealing of the sons of God... the creation itself also will be delivered from the bondage of corruption into the glorious liberty of the children of God." These verses reveal that creation, subjected to decay and corruption because of humanity's fall, longs for the day when God's children will step into their full identity as sons and daughters of God. This transformation will bring freedom and restoration not only to humanity but also to all creation, breaking its bondage and restoring it to its intended state.

*Through His victory over sin and death, Jesus reversed the curse that entered the world through Adam's transgression. However, the fulfillment of this restoration is still unfolding, as creation eagerly anticipates the revealing of God's sons, who will usher in its ultimate liberation. In this, Jesus' resurrection not only secured eternal life for believers but also established hope for the renewal of the entire created order, pointing to a place where corruption will be replaced with incorruption and mortality will be swallowed up by life.*

## Sixth Plague - Boils

Pharaoh, in his continued defiance and hardened heart, refused to release the Israelites so they could worship their God. He remained resolute in his rebellion against God's command. As a result of his stubbornness, the Lord sent yet another plague upon Egypt, The details of this plague are recorded in Exodus 9:8-9 (NKJV): "So the Lord said to Moses and Aaron, 'Take for yourselves handfuls of ashes from a furnace, and let Moses scatter it toward the heavens in the sight of Pharaoh. And it will become fine dust in all the land of Egypt, and it will cause boils that break out in sores on man and beast throughout all the land of Egypt.'"

**Sixth plague in Adam**

God created Adam and Eve as perfect beings, reflecting His divine image and possessing life in complete harmony with Him. This perfection not only encompassed their spiritual connection to God but also extended to their physical well-being, free from pain, sickness, and death. They were designed to embody God's goodness and glory, crowned with honor and destined to live in fellowship with their Creator.

However, through their transgression in the Garden of Eden, Adam and Eve entered into the corruption of both body and spirit. As a result, suffering and pain became part of the human experience. This consequence is recorded in Genesis 3:16 (NKJV): "In pain you shall bring forth children." While this statement specifically addresses Eve, it also symbolizes the broader introduction of pain into humanity, a direct consequence of the spiritual death caused by separation from God.

This declaration was not merely about childbirth but signified the beginning of physical suffering, emotional distress, and mortality for all of humanity. The body, once adorned with God's crown of glory and free from corruption, now bore the marks of death, pain, sickness, and ultimately decay to death. What was originally designed to reflect the beauty and perfection of God became subject to weakness, decay, and brokenness, illustrating the far-reaching effects of death on the body.

The loss of divine perfection caused humanity to fall from a state of glory and honor to one of frailty and vulnerability. The image of God, though not entirely erased, was marred, and the physical body, which was meant to carry the fullness of God's goodness, now carried the weight of suffering. This shift serves as a reminder of the consequences of transgression and the need for restoration.

**Sixth plague reversed**

The first mention of the word "pain" in the Bible appears in Genesis 3:16 (NKJV): "I will greatly multiply your sorrow and your conception; In pain you shall bring forth children." This occurred after Adam and Eve's transgression in the Garden of Eden, with pain specifically tied to childbirth pointing to the death in the body which is pain and sickness. Similarly, the first mention of the word "heal" is found in Genesis 20:17 (NKJV): "So Abraham prayed to God; and God healed Abimelech, his wife, and his female servants. Then they bore children." Here, healing is also linked to childbirth, representing restoration and renewal on the body.

The womb of a woman, the very place where human life begins is also the place where pain was first introduced into humanity in transgression. It was here, in the origin of human life, that the effects of sin manifested through pain and suffering. Yet, in this same place where pain was introduced, God also chose to introduce healing. This profound truth is reflected in Genesis 20:17

(NKJV). Through Abraham's intercession, God restored Abimelech's household, enabling them to bear children. This act of healing, connected to childbirth, foreshadowed God's ultimate plan to bring restoration and wholeness to humanity.

The deeper meaning of this healing is embedded in the name Abimelech, which originates from the Hebrew words "Ab" meaning Father and "Melech" meaning King. This points to the healing that comes through God the Father and the King, Jesus Christ. It reflects the spiritual reality that the restoration of humanity is accomplished through Christ, who is both the Son of God and the King of Kings. This truth is further emphasized in Isaiah 53:5 (NKJV): "But He was wounded for our transgressions, He was bruised for our iniquities; the chastisement for our peace was upon Him, and by His stripes we are healed." Through Christ's sacrifice, humanity was offered healing on the body.

Additionally, The salvation of God, symbolized by the name Jesus, which means "Salvation" in Hebrew, began its work on earth in the very place where pain and suffering were first introduced - the womb. After Eve's disobedience, the curse of pain in childbirth was pronounced (Genesis 3:16), marking the beginning of pain resulting in death of the body. However, God's redemptive plan started in the womb of Mary, who conceived by the Holy Spirit, as described in Matthew 1:20 (NKJV): "Joseph, son of David, do not be afraid to take to you Mary your wife, for that which is conceived in her is of the Holy Spirit."

*In this, God's plan for our redemption is revealed. The pain introduced through the womb as a consequence of sin is reversed in the healing through Jesus Christ. It is in Him that humanity finds restoration, as He bore their transgressions and made a way for healing of our being.*

## Seventh Plague - Hail

Pharaoh's heart remained hardened, and he continued to resist God's command to release the Israelites so they could go and worship Him. This time, God instructed Moses to deliver a warning and declare the coming of a devastating plague of hail. As recorded in Exodus 9:22 (NKJV): "Then the Lord said to Moses, 'Stretch out your hand toward heaven, that there may be hail in all the land of Egypt - on man, on beast, and on every herb of the field, throughout the land of Egypt.'" In obedience to God's command, Moses stretched out his hand, and the heavens unleashed a mighty storm of hail accompanied by fire, striking down everything left exposed in the fields.

Before the plague was sent, God, in His mercy, gave the Egyptians an opportunity to believe in His word and take precautions to protect their livestock and servants. Those who feared the word of the Lord heeded the warning and brought their animals and workers indoors, sparing them from harm. However, those who disregarded the word of the Lord and left their livestock and servants in the fields faced devastating losses, as the hailstorm killed both man and beast and destroyed crops throughout Egypt.

## Seventh plague in Adam

In Genesis 3:15 (NKJV), God pronounced judgment upon the serpent following its deception of Adam and Eve, which led to humanity's fall. The verse declares: "And I will put enmity between you and the woman, and between your seed and her Seed; He shall bruise your head, and you shall bruise His heel." This pronouncement marked the beginning of divine judgment against Satan and carried profound prophetic significance.

Throughout Scripture, examples illustrate how God's judgments are executed and His acceptance demonstrated. In 1 Kings 18:36-38 (NKJV), Elijah called upon God, and fire descended from heaven, signifying God's power and His acceptance of Elijah's offering while serving as judgment against the followers of Baal. Similarly, in Deuteronomy 4:26 (NKJV), God declared, "I call heaven and earth to witness against you this day," emphasizing that heaven and earth bear witness to His covenant and judgments. Likewise, the hailstones of the seventh plague in Egypt, which fell from heaven to earth, symbolize divine judgment and parallel the judgment pronounced upon Satan and Adam.

The judgment in Genesis 3:15 was directed at Satan, who had used the serpent as an instrument to deceive humanity. This deception resulted in the loss of humanity's God-given authority and dominion over the earth. However, the judgment was not merely about the defeat of Satan and the destruction of his works; it also carried a prophetic declaration concerning Adam's identity as a son of God. Luke 3:38 (NKJV) affirms

Adam's divine sonship, stating, "Adam, the son of God." As God's son, Adam was created as a prince within God's kingdom, entrusted with dominion over all creation.

In this judgment, God foretold humanity's ultimate victory over Satan, to be achieved through the Seed of the woman. This Seed would crush the serpent's head, signifying the complete defeat of Satan's authority and power. The phrase, "He shall bruise your head," proclaims the restoration of humanity's authority and dominion, fulfilling God's design for mankind as His children and restoring the divine glory for which Adam was created. This judgment not only condemns Satan but also prophesies the redemption and triumph of humanity through God's redemptive plan.

**Seventh plague reversed**

In John 9:39 (NKJV), Jesus declared, "For judgment I have come into this world, that those who do not see may see, and that those who see may be made blind." This statement highlights the purpose of Christ's coming-for judgment and to bring clarity to those blinded by sin and to reveal the truth to those who were lost. What humanity, through Adam, failed to achieve, they could now attain through Jesus Christ, the Last Adam.

The judgment on Satan and Adam was complete, Jesus Christ was judged while hanging on the cross witnessed between heaven and earth. In that moment, Humanity in Last Adam crushed the head of Satan under His feet and then He gave up His spirit, accomplishing the restoration of the authority and dominion that Adam had forfeited. Through His sacrificial death, Jesus opened the way for humanity to be reconciled to God, not merely as a distant deity but as a loving Father.

This restoration is unveiled in scripture as the transformation of humanity's spiritual sight. Those who were once blind to God's identity as Father now have the ability to see Him in that light. Those who previously recognized God as a sovereign authority are now invited to know Him intimately as their Father. In this profound act of redemption, Jesus restored the sonship of mankind that was lost in Adam, enabling mankind to exercise their identity as children of God, walking in the fullness of His authority and dominion.

*The judgment of hail symbolizes the judgment that fell upon humanity, which was fulfilled for mankind through Jesus Christ to restore authority by defeating and crushing the head of Satan.*

## Eighth Plague - Locusts

Pharaoh continued to harden his heart and remained defiant, refusing to release the Israelites so they could go and worship the Lord their God. Despite witnessing the earlier plagues and the devastation they brought upon Egypt, his stubbornness persisted. Pharaoh's unyielding attitude resulted in God sending Moses and Aaron to confront him once more, delivering a solemn warning of yet another plague that would come upon the land.

The Lord, through Moses, declared the impending judgment as recorded in Exodus 10:4-5 (NKJV): "If you refuse to let My people go, behold, tomorrow I will bring locusts into your territory. And they shall cover the face of the earth, so that no one will be able to see the earth; and they shall eat the residue of what is left, which remains to you from the hail, and they shall eat every tree which grows up for you out of the field."

**Eighth plague in Adam**

In Genesis 3:15-16 (NKJV), after God pronounced judgment upon the serpent and foretold the pain that Eve would endure during childbirth, He addressed Adam in the book of Genesis 3:17-19 (NKJV), God said: "Cursed is the ground for your sake;

In toil you shall eat of it all the days of your life. Both thorns and thistles it shall bring forth for you, and you shall eat the herb of the field. In the sweat of your face you shall eat bread till you return to the ground, for out of it you were taken; for dust you are, And to dust you shall return."

Before their transgression, Adam and Eve were free to eat from every tree in the Garden of Eden except the tree of the knowledge of good and evil. Their sustenance, however, did not depend on the food they ate. They lived by the breath of life that God had breathed into Adam, and the food was given to them as a source of enjoyment rather than necessity. Their life was rooted in the spirit of God, which sustained them in perfect harmony with their Creator.

However, after their disobedience, they experienced spiritual death, meaning they no longer lived by the Spirit of God but became dependent on physical food for survival. This shift reflected their fallen state, as their existence was now tied to the ground from which they were taken. God did not curse Adam, as he was made in God's image. Instead, God cursed the ground for Adam's sake.

The food that humans would now labor for, drawn from the cursed ground, this parallels the food that is destroyed by the Locusts in Egypt. Food became both a source of sustenance and a reminder of their fallen condition. "*The food that humans consume ultimately takes them back to the place from which it came.*" Humanity, once sustained by God's Spirit, was now sustained by the earth, to which they would ultimately return to death with pain and sickness of the thorns and thistles.

**Eighth plague reversed**

Many of Jesus' disciples followed Him not only because of the miracles He performed but also because He provided them with physical food. In the Gospel of John 6:26-27 (NKJV), Jesus addressed this motivation, saying, "Most assuredly, I say to you, you seek Me, not because you saw the signs, but because you ate of the loaves and were filled. Do not labor for the food which perishes, but for the food which endures to everlasting life, which the Son of Man will give you." Through this statement, Jesus shifted their focus from temporary, earthly needs to eternal, spiritual sustenance that only He could provide.

Jesus then referred to Moses and the manna given to the Israelites in the wilderness, which physically sustained them but could not give eternal life. He contrasted this with Himself, metaphorically identifying as the true "Bread of Life." In John 6:35, 50-51 (NKJV), Jesus declared, "I am the bread of life. This is the bread which comes down from heaven, that one may eat of it and not die. I am the living bread which came down from heaven. If anyone eats of this bread, he will live forever; and the bread that I shall give is My flesh, which I shall give for the life of the world." This profound statement revealed that Jesus Himself was the spiritual nourishment required for *"The Life eternal"* (Zoe life). However, this teaching proved difficult for many to accept and they walk with Him no more.

In light of this teaching, Jesus not only declared Himself as the "Bread of Life" but also instituted a covenant to symbolize this truth. On the night before His betrayal by Judas Iscariot, Jesus established the Last Supper as a sacred act of remembrance. As recorded in Matthew 26:26-28 (NKJV): "Jesus took bread, blessed and broke it, and gave it to the disciples and said, 'Take, eat; this is My body.' Then He took the cup, and gave thanks, and gave it to them, saying, 'Drink from it, all of you. For this is My blood of the new covenant.'"

*Just as "the food that humans consume ultimately returns them to the place from which it came," when humanity partakes of the bread from heaven "Jesus Christ" He assures that He will lead them back to the place from which He came, the Father.*

## Ninth Plague - Darkness

Due to Pharaoh's continued stubbornness and refusal to release the Israelites, God sent another plague through Moses. As recorded in Exodus 10:21 (NKJV): "Then the Lord said to Moses, 'Stretch out your hand toward heaven, that there may be darkness over the land of Egypt, darkness which may even be felt.'" In obedience to God's command, Moses stretched out his hand, and a thick, tangible darkness fell upon the entire land of Egypt.

This oppressive darkness lasted for three days, as described in Exodus 10:23 (NKJV): "They did not see one another; nor did anyone rise from his place for three days." The plague was so severe that the Egyptians were immobilized, unable to move or see each other, symbolizing not only physical darkness on people but also blindness upon the land.

**Ninth plague in Adam**

The moment God declared the state of humanity and foretold the consequences of their transgression, He sent Adam and Eve out of the Garden of Eden, severing their access to the tree of life. This pivotal event is recorded in Genesis 3:22-23 (NKJV): "Then the Lord God said, 'Behold, the man has become like one of Us, to know good and evil. And now, lest he put out his hand and take also of the tree of life, and eat, and live forever', therefore the Lord God sent him out of the garden of Eden to till the ground from which he was taken."

Adam, who once dwelled in the light of God's presence, clothed in divine glory and living in perfect harmony with his Creator, was now banished into a world of darkness and death. The garden, which had been a place of safety, peace, and abundance, was no longer accessible. Instead, Adam stepped into a hostile and unfamiliar wilderness, a world tainted by sin and filled with dangers.

From Adam's perspective, the transition must have been terrifying. He was stripped of the crown of glory that surrounded him, a covering that symbolized God's presence and protection. Now, he faced life outside the presence of God, exposed to the harsh realities of a fallen world. This wilderness was not only a physical place of toil and struggle but also a spiritual realm where darkness reigned. It was the same earth where Satan and his fallen angels, referred to as the sons of God in Genesis 6, had been cast down, roaming with destructive intent to corrupt humanity and oppose God's purposes.

Moreover, the beasts of the field, which once peacefully coexisted with Adam in the garden, now represented a threat, no longer tamed or harmless but ready to devour and dominate. The natural order had been disrupted, and Adam faced the weight of physical survival, laboring by the sweat of his brow to produce food from the cursed ground. The loss of the light of God's presence left Adam in a state of spiritual and physical darkness, a darkness he had never experienced before, as God's radiance had previously been his constant covering in the garden.

At last, the darkness of darkness covered humanity, a deep spiritual darkness enveloped mankind, which is severing their intimate relationship with God. Once able to see Him as a loving Father, they now viewed Him only as a distant and sovereign God.

**Ninth plague reversed**

After Jesus was betrayed by Judas Iscariot in the Garden of Gethsemane, He was arrested, tried, and sentenced to be crucified. On the cross, during His suffering, Jesus experienced a profound moment of separation, where for the first time, He personally addressed the Father as God instead of Father for the very first time. This is recorded in Matthew 27:45-46 (NKJV): “Now from the sixth hour until the ninth hour there was darkness over all the land. 46 And about the ninth hour Jesus cried out with a loud voice, saying, ‘Eli, Eli, lama sabachthani?’ that is, ‘My God, My God, why have You forsaken Me?’”

At that moment, Jesus willingly stepped into the depths of human darkness and alienation caused by sin - the very condition in which Adam found himself after the fall, seeing the Father not as a loving Father but as a distant God. This darkness covered the earth for three hours while Jesus was hanging on the cross, symbolizing the separation and judgment that Jesus endured as He bore the sins as humanity. On the cross, Jesus entered the same state of darkness that humanity inherited through Adam’s fall, experiencing the same weight of separation from the Father to redeem mankind.

Jesus had earlier prophesied about His death and burial in Matthew 12:40 (NKJV): "For as Jonah was three days and three nights in the belly of the great fish, so will the Son of Man be three days and three nights in the heart of the earth." This foreshadowed not only His time in the grave but also His descent into the darkness of death - the same darkness Adam entered after transgression and the symbolic three days of darkness during the plagues in Egypt. These parallels highlight the extent of the darkness that Jesus endured to restore humanity's relationship with God.

However, despite the anguish and separation He felt, Jesus did not die in despair. Before breathing His last, He once again addressed God as Father, restoring the intimate relationship that had been severed through sin. In Luke 23:46 (NKJV), it is written: "And when Jesus had cried out with a loud voice, He said, 'Father, into Your hands I commit My spirit.' Having said this, He breathed His last." This final declaration as Father signified the restoration of sonship and fellowship, fulfilling God's plan to reconcile humanity back to Himself.

The apostle Paul reinforces this truth in Galatians 2:20 (NKJV): "I have been crucified with Christ; it is no longer I who live, but Christ lives in me." Through Christ's death, humanity is crucified with Him, meaning Jesus entered humanity's utter darkness to redeem them and pull them out of separation into light. Now, in Jesus Christ, humanity can approach God not as a distant God but as Abba, Father, restoring the relationship lost through Adam and securing eternal fellowship with Him.

*Jesus stepped into the depths of our darkness, saw what we saw, experienced what we experienced, and endured what we endured. Finally, He reconciled humanity to God through Himself, leading us out of the darkness and opening our eyes and causing us to see what He sees, the Father. Not only the Father but also to see others around us with the same light.*

## Tenth Plague - Death of the First born

God delivered the final and most devastating plague upon Egypt through His servant Moses, a plague that struck down the firstborn in every household. This judgment fell upon everyone, from the firstborn of Pharaoh, who sat in authority on the throne, to the firstborn of the lowest captives confined in prison dungeons. This event is recorded in Exodus 12:29 (NKJV): "And it came to pass at midnight that the Lord struck all the firstborn in the land of Egypt, from the firstborn of Pharaoh who sat on his throne to the firstborn of the captive who was in the dungeon, and all the firstborn of livestock."

Overwhelmed by the severity of the plague, Pharaoh summoned Moses and Aaron during the night and relented, finally allowing the Israelites to leave. As recorded in Exodus 12:31-32 (NKJV):

"Then he called for Moses and Aaron by night, and said, 'Rise, go out from among my people, both you and the children of Israel. And go, serve the Lord as you have said. Also take your flocks and your herds, as you have said, and be gone; and bless me also.'"

**Tenth plague in Adam**

Scripture reveals that Adam lived for nine hundred and thirty years, as recorded in Genesis 5:5 (NKJV): “So all the days that Adam lived were nine hundred and thirty years; and he died.” Although Adam experienced spiritual death immediately on the day he disobeyed God and ate from the Tree of the Knowledge of Good and Evil, his physical death occurred much later, marking the culmination of a gradual process of deterioration. This process began when he lost the crown of glory that once surrounded him, leaving him exposed to corruption, vulnerability, and decay, which ultimately led to his physical demise.

God’s original design for Adam, however, was not death but eternal life, both spiritually and physically. Adam was created in God’s image, meant to live in perpetual communion with his Creator, reflecting His glory and walking in His presence. Yet, when Adam transgressed, he was severed from the spirit that gave life, resulting in a fallen state that affected not only his spirit but also his body. The loss of spiritual life initiated a chain reaction, introducing mortality and decay into the human experience.

Physical death of mankind in Adam signifies a complete separation from the original purpose for which God created mankind - to live in eternal fellowship and communion with Him. As expressed in Psalm 6:5 (NKJV): “For in death there is no remembrance of You; In the grave who will give You thanks?” This verse reflects the reality that death interrupts the ability to love, be loved by God. It emphasizes that in the grave, mankind can no longer fulfill its intended role of glorifying the Father in communion, either spiritually or physically.

**Tenth plague reversed**

He is risen! (Matthew 28:6) Yes, Jesus has risen from the dead, fulfilling what is written in Psalm 16:9-10 (NKJV): "Therefore my heart is glad, and my glory rejoices; My flesh also will rest in hope. For You will not leave my soul in Sheol, Nor will You allow Your Holy One to see corruption." This passage expresses the confidence and hope that even in physical death, the flesh can rest with the assurance of being restored to its former glory. It highlights God's promise that He would not allow His Holy One, Jesus Christ, to experience decay, affirming the resurrection as a divine act of power and victory over death.

The resurrection of Jesus was not just a personal triumph but also a transformative act for all humanity. Scripture declares that believers have been crucified with Christ on His cross, as stated in Galatians 2:20 (NKJV): "I have been crucified with Christ; it is no longer I who live, but Christ lives in me." This signifies that humanity shares in the death of Jesus, furthermore, through baptism, humanity is buried with Him, identifying fully with His death and resurrection.

When the Holy Spirit raised Jesus from the dead, as recorded in Romans 8:11 (NKJV): "the Spirit of Him who raised Jesus from the dead dwells in you, He who raised Christ from the dead will also give life to your mortal bodies through His Spirit who dwells in you,"

Humanity were also raised to new life. Not only are they raised, but they are seated with Him in heavenly places, as stated in Ephesians 2:6 (NKJV): "and raised us up together, and made us sit together in the heavenly places in Christ Jesus."

This resurrection and ascension established a restored relationship between humanity and God, binding humanity together with Jesus in His death and resurrection, enabling us to approach Him with confidence. Hebrews 4:16 (NKJV): encourages them to "come boldly to the throne of grace, that we may obtain mercy and find grace to help in time of need." Through Christ's resurrection, humanity can now call God, "Abba, Father," as expressed in Romans 8:15 (NKJV): "you received the Spirit of adoption by whom we cry out, 'Abba, Father.'" This adoption into God's family affirms their identity as children of God and heirs to His promises.

Moreover, Jesus is declared the firstborn among many brethren, as noted in Romans 8:29 (NKJV): "that He might be the firstborn among many brethren." His physical resurrection in the body, not only paved the way for humanity's redemption but also reversed the curse of eternal death and separation from the Father, both spiritually and physically. Through Christ, the plague of death and its consequences has been defeated.

*Thus, the resurrection of Jesus Christ stands as the ultimate triumph, securing eternal life, restored fellowship with the Father, and dominion over creation. Through Him, humanity is not only redeemed from death but also empowered to live as sons and daughters of God, walking in freedom, boldness, and victory.*

## Summary

The ten plagues of Egypt symbolically represent the spiritual and physical losses that humanity suffered when Adam ate from the Tree of the Knowledge of Good and Evil. This act resulted in the loss of life sustained by the Spirit of God and ultimately led to physical death. Humanity, bound by these plagues, was powerless to save itself.

Jesus Christ, taking on human form, stepped into humanity's condition and personally overcame these plagues within Himself. Through His obedience, sacrificial death, and resurrection, Christ conquered sin and its consequences.

Believers, united with Christ, share in this victory, realizing they have been crucified with Him on the cross, buried with Him through baptism, and raised with Him in resurrection, they now walk in the newness of life. In Christ, they are more than conquerors, boldly proclaiming, "O Death, where is your sting? O Hades, where is your victory?" (1 Corinthians 15:55) as they stand restored in authority and eternal life.

| No | Plague | What happened to Adam | What happened in Jesus Christ |
|---|---|---|---|
| **1** | Water became Blood | Dead in the Spirit | John 2:1-11 - Marriage at Cana, Water turned to Wine (represents blood of Jesus) |
| **2** | Frogs | Unclean Spirit | John 14:16-17 - Promise of Holy Spirit |
| **3** | Lice | Lost the crown of Glory on the body | 2 Corinthians 3:18 - We Beholding His Glory |
| **4** | Flies | Beelzebub - Lord of Flies, under Satan's rulership | Luke 10:18-19 - Authority Given to us in Jesus Christ |
| **5** | Livestock | All creation subjected to death | Romans 8:19, 21 - Liberty to be declared to all creation in Jesus Christ |
| **6** | Boils | Pain & Suffering | Isaiah 53:5 - He took our pain and suffering |

| | | | |
|---|---|---|---|
| **7** | Hail | Judgment on Satan and Adam (heaven & earth as witness) | John 9:39 - For Judgment Jesus came to this world (hanging between heaven and earth) |
| **8** | Locusts | Curse on the Ground/Food (Food of life) | John 6:35 - Jesus, Bread of Life from the Heaven |
| **9** | Darkness | Total separation from the Father and to see Him as God | Luke 23:46 - Jesus called Him "Father" after entering through the darkness of Adam |
| **10** | Death of the Firstborn | Death of Adam (Firstborn) | Matthew 28:6 - Resurrection of Jesus Christ (Firstborn) |

**Take Away**

The plagues and hardships experienced in this life are not eternal, for God, in His infinite love and mercy, provided redemption through His only begotten Son, Jesus Christ. Jesus, fully God, took on human flesh and entered into the very condition of humanity to reverse the effects of sin and the curse brought upon mankind through Adam's disobedience. As stated in John 3:16 (NKJV): "For God so loved the world that He gave His only begotten Son, that whoever believes in Him should not perish but have everlasting life."

Jesus came not only to redeem humanity but also to restore everything that was lost through Adam's fall. In Adam, humanity experienced separation from God, spiritual death, and the introduction of pain, sickness, toil, and mortality. However, Jesus, often referred to as the Last Adam in Scripture, stepped into the brokenness of this world and overcame every form of defeat that humanity had endured. Through His obedience, sacrifice on the cross, and resurrection, Jesus conquered sin, death, and every curse that followed the fall.

This victory is not limited to spiritual restoration but also extends to every area of life that was affected by the fall, symbolized by the plagues that came upon Egypt, which metaphorically reflect the losses humanity suffered in Adam. Jesus Christ triumphed over these plagues by becoming the ultimate sacrifice, bearing the weight of sin and death, and becoming our eternal life and restoration.

Now, through faith in Jesus, believers have victory over every plague that resulted from Adam's disobedience. As written in 1 Corinthians 15:57 (NKJV): "But thanks be to God, who gives us the victory through our Lord Jesus Christ." This victory is not temporary or incomplete but eternal and all-encompassing, allowing believers to walk in freedom, healing, and restoration as sons and daughters of God.

Through Christ's finished work, humanity no longer has to live under the curse but can experience life in abundance, walking in authority and dominion that was originally intended for Adam. By faith in Christ, believers can confidently declare triumph over sin, sickness, and death, standing firm in the promise of eternal victory and restored fellowship with the Father God.

## My Reflection

*My seventy-eight-year-old mother lives in India with my sister. One day, I received a devastating call from my sister, telling me that my mother had been admitted to the hospital in critical condition. Her lungs and k idneys had completely shut down, and she had been unresponsive for two days. The doctors said there was nothing more they could do except place her on irreversible life support to sustain her. With a heavy heart, we were asked to sign the papers to authorize the process. Fighting back tears and grief, I agreed to sign the papers just before boarding an emergency flight to India.*

*As my family and I prepared for the twenty-two-hour journey, my friends came together, falling on their knees in prayer. During the first sixteen-hour flight, we landed in Dubai for a transit connection. My heart raced as I called my sister from Dubai to check on my mother's condition, fearing the worst. To my astonishment, my sister shared the incredible news that my mother's failed k idneys had suddenly started functioning again. The doctors had confirmed that she no longer needed life support.*

*Filled with hope and gratitude, we boarded our connecting flight and finally landed in Chennai, India. As soon as we arrived, I called my sister again to check on my mom, and she told me that after a few days since she became unresponsive, my mom had started responding. I was completely overwhelmed. I had never heard of failed organs suddenly coming back to life. It was nothing short of a miracle.*

*Through this experience, I was reminded of God's faithfulness and His desire for us to live a life filled with joy, blessings, and abundance in Him. He showed me that we can be victorious over death and all its byproducts, including pain and sickness. My mother's miraculous recovery was a testimony of how we can live in God's power to restore life, and it strengthened my faith in Him.*

# Chapter - 6
# CONCLUSION

## The journey to seeing through the Father's eyes

From the earliest records of divine encounters to the sacred texts preserved through generations, the quest to know and relate to God has shaped civilizations, guided faith, and defined human identity. However, this journey has often been obscured by traditions, doctrines, and misinterpretations that have distorted the true intent of scripture. This book has sought to realign our perspective, not merely by exploring historical and theological insights, but by inviting us to see the scriptures through the eyes of the Father.

## God's True Desire: Relationship, Not Religion

At the heart of scripture lies an unchanging truth - God's desire is not for legalistic obedience, but for an intimate relationship with His children. The names, attributes, and revelations of God throughout history have often been viewed through the lens of power, sovereignty, and divine authority. Yet, Jesus introduced a radical shift - revealing God not merely as "Lord" or "Judge," but as "Father." This perspective changes everything. It moves us from a transactional understanding of God to a relational one, where obedience is not driven by obligation but by love.

## The Scriptures: A Divine Roadmap

This book has explored the Bible's historical development, doctrinal interpretations, and theological insights to uncover its true purpose, not as a rulebook, but as a testimony that leads humanity to Christ. Jesus Himself declared, "You search the Scriptures because you think they give you eternal life. But the

Scriptures point to me!" (John 5:39, NLT). This truth reframes the way we read and interpret scripture. The Bible is not merely a record of laws, covenants, and prophetic messages; it is a revelation of the Father's love, fully expressed in Jesus Christ.

## The Law: A Guidepost, Not the Destination

One of the greatest misunderstandings throughout religious history has been the role of the Law. The Law was never meant to be the final standard of righteousness, but a signpost leading to Christ. It served as a mirror, revealing humanity's inability to attain His standards and pointing toward the necessity of Father God's favor.

Moses, the great lawgiver, embodied this truth - he could lead the people to the border of the Promised Land, but he himself could not take them in. That role was fulfilled by Joshua (Yeshua), whose very name foreshadows Jesus, the One who brings us into the fullness of God's promises. In Christ, the burden of striving under the Law is lifted, and the invitation to live in grace is extended.

## The Ten Plagues: A Symbol of Redemption

The story of the Ten Plagues of Egypt is often viewed solely as a demonstration of God's judgment against Pharaoh. However, a deeper look reveals that these plagues symbolize the spiritual and physical consequences of humanity's fall through Adam - and their ultimate reversal through Christ. Each plague represents an aspect of what was lost in Adam: purity, dominion, authority, and life itself. Yet, through Jesus, every loss has been restored.

From the water turning to blood (symbolizing spiritual death) to the death of the firstborn (pointing to Christ's sacrifice and resurrection), these events serve as a prophetic narrative of redemption. Jesus, as the Last Adam, took upon Himself the full weight of sin, darkness, and death so that humanity could be restored to its original purpose - walking in the fullness of life as sons and daughters of God.

## Final Reflections: Seeing Through the Eyes of Christ

Ultimately, the journey through this book has led to one central truth: to truly understand scripture, we must see through the eyes of Jesus. He is the perfect revelation of the Father (John 14:9), the fulfillment of the Law

(Matthew 5:17), and the embodiment of the Word (John 1:14). When we interpret scripture through Him, we move beyond religion into relationship, beyond law into grace, and beyond knowledge into intimacy with God.

This journey is not just an academic or theological pursuit—it is deeply personal, transformation comes not through rigid adherence to rules, but through understanding Him. When we shift from seeing God through the lens of fear to embracing Him as a loving Father, everything changes. Our faith deepens, our burdens are lifted, and our lives are transformed.

## Final Invitation: Walking in the Light of Christ

As we conclude this journey through the scriptures, theology, and divine revelation, it is important to reflect on the overarching themes and insights that have emerged. This book has sought to redefine how we engage with scripture - not merely as a collection of laws, doctrines, or historical events, but as the living revelation of Father God's heart toward humanity.

As you close this book, the question remains: How will you approach scripture moving forward?

- Will you see it through the eyes of tradition or through the eyes of revelation?
- Will you approach God as a distant deity or as a loving Father?
- Will you live under the weight of the Law or in the freedom of Grace?

The choice is yours.

May this journey inspire you to see the Bible as God sees it, to embrace the fullness of His revelation in Christ, and to walk in the light, truth, and love of the Father, now and forever.

Amen.

# FUTURE VOLUMES
# A CONTINUED EXPLORATION

The upcoming volumes in this series will continue to explore profound spiritual themes, delving deeper into the timeless truths of faith, humanity, and the divine. Each book will build upon the foundation laid in the first volume, offering fresh perspectives and insights that inspire readers to grow in their understanding of God's purpose and their relationship with Him.

Through these future works, readers will journey through the complexities of life, addressing essential questions of identity, faith, and shift your view of spiritual living. The series will also explore practical and spiritual dimensions of living a life rooted in divine principles, fostering a deeper connection with the Creator and with others around us.

Designed to guide readers toward greater clarity, wisdom, and transformation, these volumes aim to illuminate the path to spiritual fulfillment and understanding. With each volume, the series aspires to nurture a more intimate and dynamic relationship with God, equipping readers to start living the eternal life of heaven on earth.

# ABOUT THE AUTHOR

Satish Mylapore, a passionate seeker of spiritual truth, emerges as a voice dedicated to unveiling the profound depths of understanding the Father's heart. With a lifelong commitment to personal transformation and spiritual awakening, Satish draws upon his rich experiences and meditations to illuminate timeless wisdom for those on the journey of faith and inner discovery.

Satish's spiritual path has been shaped by a deep, personal relationship with God and an unwavering thirst for truth. His exploration of spiritual systems and practices is rooted in a desire to bridge the gap between divine teachings and daily life. For Satish, spirituality is not confined to rituals or places of worship but is a way of living with authenticity, grace, and intention - reflecting the heart of Jesus Christ on earth.

In addition to being an author, Satish brings his unique perspective to his professional life in the Information Technology industry. He believes in integrating spiritual principles with everyday challenges to create a life filled with purpose, compassion, and gratitude. His teachings inspire readers to live intentionally and to experience God as a loving Father in every moment of their lives.

Satish treasures time with his beloved wife, Sathya Priya, and their two children, Josiah and Josana. He enjoys engaging in meaningful conversations that nurture the soul and strengthen bonds. He invites readers to connect with him at satish.mylapore@gmail.com, fostering a community of shared growth and spiritual exploration.

Satish's mission is to guide individuals to uncover the spiritual truths, live in harmony with the Father, and radiate love and light to the world. Through his writings, he aims to inspire readers to see God not as distant, but as a present and loving companion throughout their earthly journey.